MAKE it WORK!

ANCIENT ROME

WITHDRAWN

Author: Peter Chrisp

Consultant: Simon James B.Sc., Ph.D
The British Museum, London

Series creator: Andrew Haslam

TWO CAN ™

PRINCETON ■ LONDON

Published in the United States and Canada by
Two-Can Publishing LLC
234 Nassau Street
Princeton, NJ 08542

www.two-canpublishing.com

© 2001, 1996 Two-Can Publishing

For information on Two-Can books and multimedia,
call 1-609-921-6700, fax 1-609-921-3349, or visit our Web site at
http://www.two-canpublishing.com

Editor: Jacqueline McCann
Art direction and design: Helen McDonagh
Managing Editor: Christine Morley
Commissioned photography: Jon Barnes
Additional photography: John Englefield and Ray Moller
Picture Research: Lyndsey Price
Production: Joya Bart-Plange
Model-maker: Melanie Williams
Additional model-makers: Peter Griffiths, Corina Holzherr, Paul Holzherr

'Two-Can' is a trademark of Two-Can Publishing.
Two-Can Publishing is a division of Zenith Entertainment Ltd,
43-45 Dorset Street, London W1H 4AB

hc ISBN 1-58728-309-3
sc   ISBN 1-58728-303-4

hc 1 2 3 4 5 6 7 8 9 10 02 01 00
sc   1 2 3 4 5 6 7 8 9 10 02 01 00

Photographic credits: AKG London/Erich Lessing: p38, p51, p59; Ancient Art & Architecture Collection: p49;
British Musuem: p42; BM/The Bridgeman Art Library: p60; C M Dixon: p12, p25, p44; Elsevier Archive/
Atlas of the Roman World: p16; Michael Holford: p19, p28, p32, p36, p40, p48; Peter Clayton: p50;
Planet Earth Pictures: p4 (tr); Scala: p4 (bl), p24; Tony Stone/Jean Pragan: p60; Zefa: p46.

With thanks to the models: Sarah Abbott, Nadine Case, Francesca Collins, Tracy Ann Francis, Sammie-Jo Gold,
Matthew Harper, Aaron Haseley, Amanda Kwakye, Dean Newell, Jonathan Page, Davina Plummer,
Robin Richards, Sean Richardson, James Sayle, Jamie White, Daniel Wright, Jia Jia Wang and Ali Issaq.
and to Wixs Lane School in Clapham, London.

Printed in Hong Kong by Wing King Tong

Contents

The ancient Romans

All human beings need food and shelter to survive. They also need a system of beliefs that gives shape and meaning to their lives. Throughout history, people have developed different ways of meeting these basic needs. By studying the people of **ancient Rome**, we can learn how they used the resources around them to create a sophisticated way of life, many traces of which survive to this day.

IN THIS BOOK, we look at the **civilization** of the ancient Romans, a people of Italian origin. Two thousand years ago, they conquered most of Europe, North Africa, and the Middle East, creating one of the biggest empires in the world.

△ *Underwater archaeologists have explored many Roman shipwrecks in the Mediterranean Sea.*

WE KNOW ABOUT THE ROMANS thanks to the many books and letters that have survived from their time. The remains of Roman cities, villas, forts, and shipwrecks help **archaeologists** to build up a picture of daily life in ancient Rome.

THE EARLIEST ROMAN HISTORY is not known, so the Romans used the ancient legend of Romulus and Remus to explain how their city was founded. Legend has it that they were the twin sons of Mars, the god of war. They were abandoned at birth and rescued by a she-wolf. Romulus later became the first ruler of Rome, and the city was named after him.

ROME was founded as a tiny farming settlement on the banks of the Tiber River. The date of its founding is traditionally given as 753 B.C. At the time, Italy was a land of many different peoples, speaking different languages. There were the **Etruscans** and Umbrians north of Rome, and Greek settlers in the south. The first Romans belonged to the **Latin**-speaking peoples of central Italy.

▽ *Today, statues of Romulus and Remus and the she-wolf can be seen all over Rome and other Italian cities.*

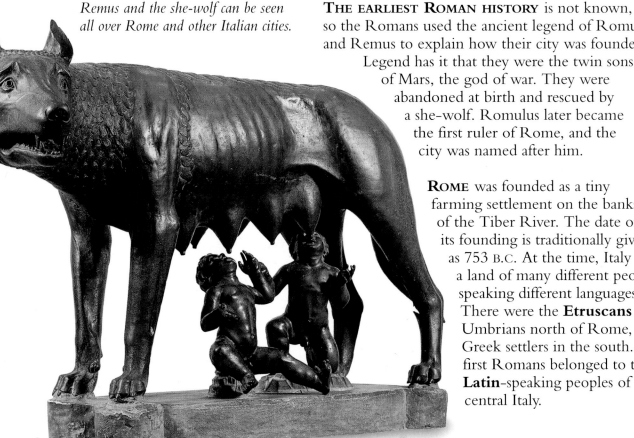

◁ *The* **fasces** *was a bundle of rods tied around an ax. It was an Etruscan symbol of power that was later used by the Romans.*

THE ETRUSCANS were a powerful people. In the 500's B.C., Rome came under their influence and was ruled by a series of Etruscan kings. The Etruscans were good builders, and they gave Rome its first large temples.

THE GREEKS were another important influence on the Romans. They founded cities around the coast of southern Italy. The Romans copied Greek buildings and sculpture, and were influenced by Greek legends and ideas.

ROMAN CIVILIZATION lasted for many centuries. To help make sense of it, we have divided it into different periods. Each period has been given a **symbol**, to show when information relates to that time. If there are no symbols, the information covers all periods.

The Republic refers to that period in Roman history when Rome was ruled by elected officials, and the Roman territory started to increase. By 27 B.C., the Republic had ended and was replaced by the rule of **emperors**. Under their rule, the Empire continued to expand. Later, the Empire was divided into two parts: the Eastern and Western Empire.

KEY FOR SYMBOLS

(eagle)	**Roman Republic** 509-27 B.C.	
(wreath)	**early imperial period** 27 B.C.-A.D. 284	
(Chi-Rho)	**late imperial period** A.D. 284-476	

THE MAKE IT WORK! way of looking at history is to ask questions about the past and to discover some of the answers by making copies of the things people made. However, you do not need to make everything in the book in order to understand the Roman way of life.

▽ *This map shows how, in Rome's earliest period, the ancient Romans were influenced by different peoples.*

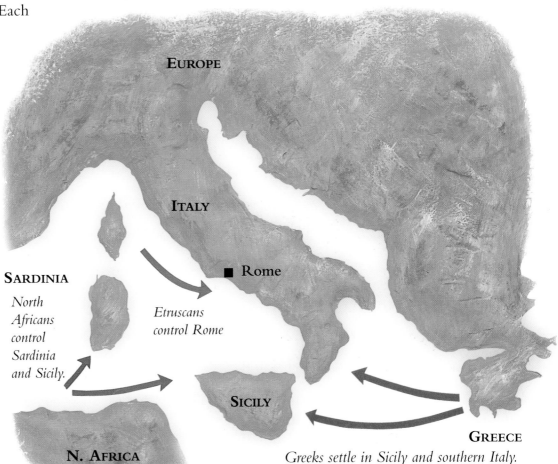

EUROPE

ITALY

SARDINIA

North Africans control Sardinia and Sicily.

■ Rome

Etruscans control Rome

SICILY

N. AFRICA

GREECE

Greeks settle in Sicily and southern Italy.

Timeline

Rome was ruled by kings until 509 B.C. After this time, the Romans set up a new form of government called the Republic. Instead of a king, the Romans were ruled by two officials called **consuls**, elected each year from among the leading **citizens**. This system lasted for almost 500 years. During this period, Rome grew from a small city to become the capital of a huge empire.

DURING THE REPUBLIC, as the Roman Empire grew, so did the size of its armies and the influence of the generals who commanded them. In the first century B.C., there were bloody wars in which rival generals fought each other for power. Eventually, only one remained: Octavian. He became the first emperor of Rome and renamed himself Augustus. He called himself the "first citizen," rather than "emperor" and pretended that he had saved the Republic. But although consuls were still elected, real power lay with the emperor.

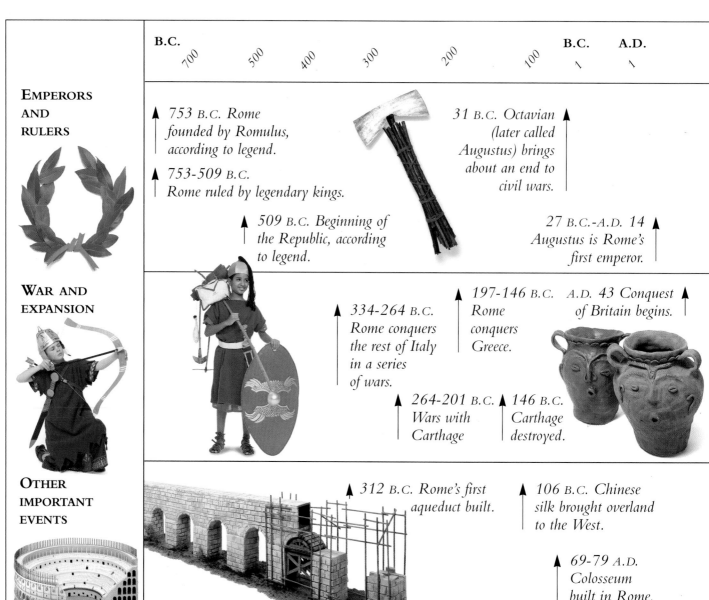

B.C. | 700 | 500 | 400 | 300 | 200 | 100 | B.C. | A.D.

EMPERORS AND RULERS

753 B.C. Rome founded by Romulus, according to legend.

753-509 B.C. Rome ruled by legendary kings.

509 B.C. Beginning of the Republic, according to legend.

31 B.C. Octavian (later called Augustus) brings about an end to civil wars.

27 B.C.-A.D. 14 Augustus is Rome's first emperor.

WAR AND EXPANSION

334-264 B.C. Rome conquers the rest of Italy in a series of wars.

264-201 B.C. Wars with Carthage

146 B.C. Carthage destroyed.

197-146 B.C. Rome conquers Greece.

A.D. 43 Conquest of Britain begins.

OTHER IMPORTANT EVENTS

312 B.C. Rome's first aqueduct built.

106 B.C. Chinese silk brought overland to the West.

69-79 A.D. Colosseum built in Rome.

Death of Jesus Christ c. A.D. 30

THE FIRST EMPEROR, AUGUSTUS, was a successful ruler. His reign lasted for over 40 years, and the Romans got used to being ruled by just one man. When Augustus died, his adopted son, Tiberius, became emperor after him. The Empire continued to grow until, in A.D. 117, it reached its greatest extent. The emperor needed people he could trust to help him rule the Empire, so he appointed governors to each of the **provinces**. Most of the army's time was spent defending the borders against foreign invaders.

THE HISTORY OF ROME is not just about emperors and wars. As time passed, many changes took place in the way that people lived. Through trade, they were introduced to new goods, such as Chinese silk. Their beliefs also changed as they came across foreign religions. The Syrians introduced them to the worship of the Sun; from Egypt they learned about the goddess **Isis**. But the religion that was to have the greatest effect was Christianity. In the A.D. 300's, this became the official religion of the Empire.

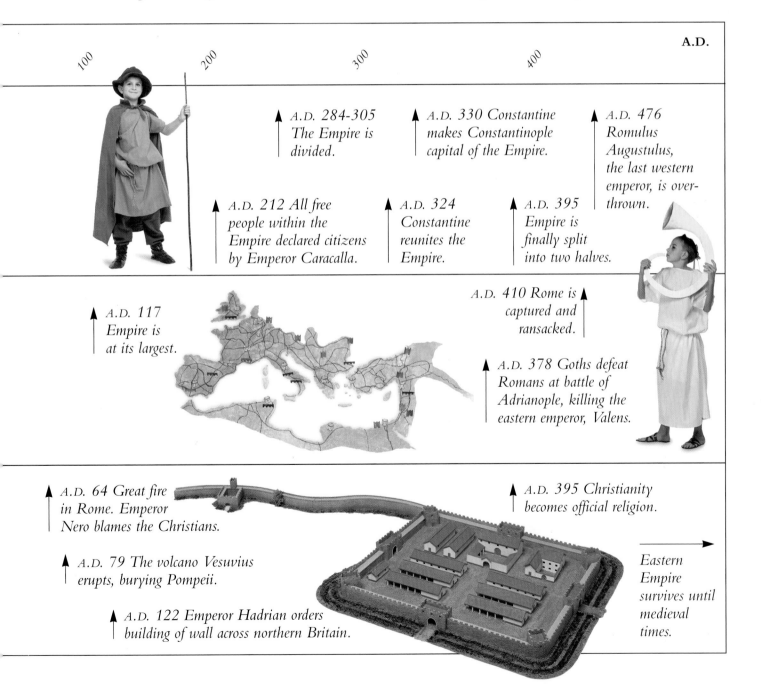

A.D.

100   200   300   400

A.D. 284-305 The Empire is divided.

A.D. 330 Constantine makes Constantinople capital of the Empire.

A.D. 476 Romulus Augustulus, the last western emperor, is over-thrown.

A.D. 212 All free people within the Empire declared citizens by Emperor Caracalla.

A.D. 324 Constantine reunites the Empire.

A.D. 395 Empire is finally split into two halves.

A.D. 117 Empire is at its largest.

A.D. 410 Rome is captured and ransacked.

A.D. 378 Goths defeat Romans at battle of Adrianople, killing the eastern emperor, Valens.

A.D. 64 Great fire in Rome. Emperor Nero blames the Christians.

A.D. 395 Christianity becomes official religion.

A.D. 79 The volcano Vesuvius erupts, burying Pompeii.

Eastern Empire survives until medieval times.

A.D. 122 Emperor Hadrian orders building of wall across northern Britain.

A conquering force

In the year A.D. 117, the Roman Empire reached its greatest size. It stretched 2,500 miles (4,000 kilometers) from east to west, 2,300 miles (3,700 kilometers) from north to south, and had a population of over 50 million.

🦅 ☽ **THE WESTERN** half of the Empire was conquered as a result of rivalry between the Romans and the people of Carthage. The Carthaginians were a powerful seafaring people in North Africa who also controlled Sardinia, parts of Sicily, and southern Spain. During a series of wars, Rome defeated Carthage and claimed its territory. The Romans later moved into northern Europe, conquering northern Spain, France, parts of Germany, and Britain.

🦅 ☽ **THE EAST** mostly came under Roman control during the last two centuries B.C. The Romans first went east to fight a people from northern Greece who were allied with Carthage. After defeating them, many more wars of conquest followed. By 30 B.C. most of the lands around the Mediterranean were part of the Roman Empire. Roman rule put an end to fighting between rival states and brought peace.

▷ *This is a map of the Empire during the A.D. 100's. Some important provinces are marked in capital letters. Provincial capitals, important cities, and army bases are given with their Roman names. You could compare the names to those on a modern map of Europe.*

BRITANNIA

Londinium

Isca

Calleva

Colonia Agrippina

GERMANIA

Mogontiacum

GAUL

Legio

IBERIA

Massilia

Lugdunum

Roma

Toletum

Ostia

ITALIA

Mediterranean Sea

Emerita Augustus

Carthago

Hispalis

Thugga

MAURETANIA

AFRICA

KEY TO SYMBOLS

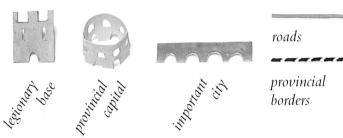

legionary base *provincial capital* *important city*

roads

- - - - - *provincial borders*

TWO LANGUAGES held the Empire together. In the west, educated people learned to speak Latin; in the east, they spoke Greek. The Romans looked down on all other languages. Foreigners who could not speak Latin or Greek were called **barbarians**, because their speech sounded to Romans like a string of meaningless "bar-bar" sounds.

ROMAN CITIZENSHIP was given to the most important people in the conquered lands. This meant that they were allowed to become Romans. Citizens had many rights denied to noncitizens. A male citizen could vote in local government, or stand for election. Becoming a citizen was like taking on a new identity: a citizen even had to take a Roman name and learn how to wear Roman clothes.

THE NUMBER OF ROMAN CITIZENS grew steadily over time. In 28 B.C., there were four million: 80 years later, the figure had risen to six million. Finally in A.D. 212, the Emperor Caracalla allowed all free men and women, including former slaves, to become citizens.

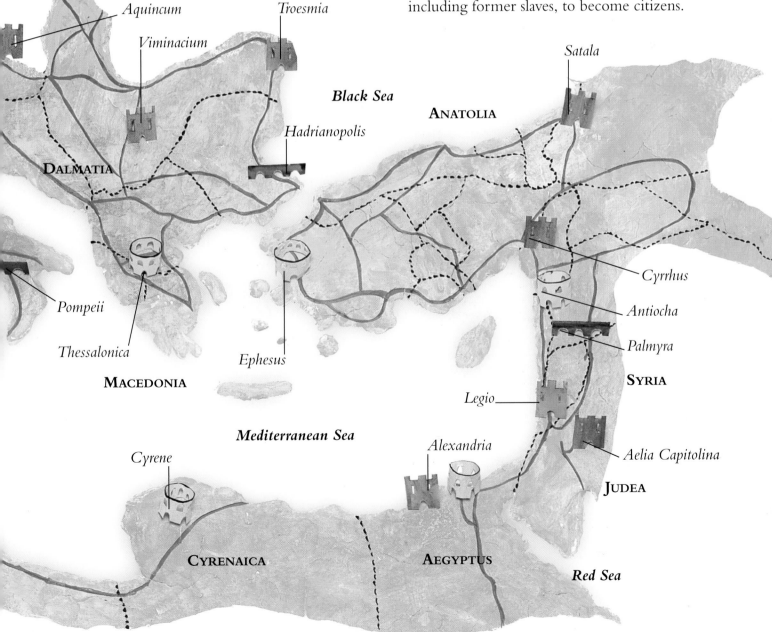

Aquincum

Viminacium

Troesmia

Satala

Black Sea

ANATOLIA

Hadrianopolis

DALMATIA

Cyrrhus

Antiocha

Pompeii

Palmyra

Thessalonica

Ephesus

SYRIA

Legio

MACEDONIA

Aelia Capitolina

Mediterranean Sea

Alexandria

JUDEA

Cyrene

CYRENAICA

AEGYPTUS

Red Sea

From emperor to slave

The people of Rome belonged to separate groups and classes, each with different rights. During the early imperial period, the most important distinction was between Roman citizens and noncitizens, or **provincials**. Citizens had more rights than provincials and even dressed differently.

SLAVES were men, women, and children who were owned as property and who were bought and sold in the market-place. Some were captured in wars, others were the children of slave parents. Household slaves could be secretaries, tutors, entertainers, cooks, or servants. These slaves were far better off than those who worked on farms or down in the mines.

double pipes

△ *A household slave who is also a musician.*

▷ *A provincial farmer from northern Europe.*

▷ *A freedman could become a successful tradesman.*

ROMAN SLAVES who had been given their freedom were called **freedmen** and **freedwomen**. Many slaves saved money and bought their freedom; others were freed by their owners as a reward for loyal service.

 PROVINCIALS, or non-citizens, had different degrees of wealth and status. Unlike slaves, they could serve in the army in special support, or "auxiliary" units. After many years of service, **auxiliaries** and their families were usually given Roman citizenship. This was one way in which the number of citizens steadily increased.

trousers were worn in the cold north

◁ *A centurion was a middle-ranking Roman citizen.*

WOMEN had fewer rights than men. They could not vote or follow careers in politics or law. Most wealthy Roman women looked after children and the home, and gave orders to slaves. However, women could own property, and some ran their own businesses. Other women played important roles as priestesses in the temples (see page 35).

✿ ✳ **THE EMPEROR** had enormous power. He was the chief priest of the Roman religion and the overall commander of Rome's armies. He appointed governors to rule the different provinces of the Empire. Statues of him stood in every city, and his face appeared on every coin.

laurel wreath

▷ *A noblewoman and priestess.*

purple **toga**

altar for making offerings to the gods

ROMAN CITIZENS were divided into different "orders" or ranks, depending on their wealth and family background. At the top were the wealthy nobles who belonged to the order of **senators**. They were the generals, chief priests, and governors of the most important provinces. Below them were **equestrians**, wealthy people who became civil servants, high-ranking officers, or governors of smaller provinces. Lower still were ordinary citizens. They ranged from **centurions** and **legionaries**, to wealthy traders and poor farmers.

△ *The emperor was the most important person in Roman society.*

Togas and tunics

Roman men, women, and children wore a simple tunic made of wool or linen, with a belt around the waist. Some had sleeves, like a T-shirt; others had armholes. This was the one item of clothing that everyone, rich and poor, wore. Women's tunics were longer than men's, reaching to below the knees.

MALE ROMAN CITIZENS were supposed to wear a **toga** in public. The toga was a huge, semicircular, woolen sheet that was wrapped around the body and arranged in folds. It took time and skill to put it on properly. Slaves and noncitizens wore the simple tunic, or *tunica*.

DIFFERENT-COLORED TOGAS were also a sign of status. Men working for election wore a pure white toga. This has given us the word *candidate,* from the Latin word *candidus* (white). **Magistrates** and the young sons of wealthy families wore a *toga praetexta,* which was white with a purple border. The emperor wore a *toga picta,* which was purple with gold embroidery.

△ *This group of senators are all wearing togas. The Roman on the far right also holds the* fasces *symbol.*

✿ ✳ **WOMEN** had a greater variety of clothing to choose from. Over the *tunica* they wore many different kinds of robes and dresses. Richer women wore clothes of brightly colored Chinese silk and Indian cotton, decorated with jewelry.

FOOTWEAR included various kinds of leather sandals. Slaves and citizens in warmer provinces wore simple sandals, like modern flip-flops. Soldiers wore stronger sandals with hobnails on the soles.

MAKE A TUNICA

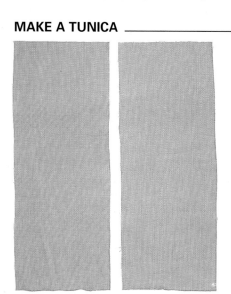

You will need: needle, thread, scissors, an old cotton sheet cut in half lengthwise, string, colored wool, long cocktail sticks, thin wire, gold paint

1 Fold over a third of the material on each piece. You could hem the edges to prevent fraying. You will need to hold the material as shown above, up to your shoulders, in the final stage.

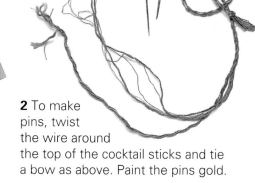

2 To make pins, twist the wire around the top of the cocktail sticks and tie a bow as above. Paint the pins gold.

3 For the belt, twist the string and long strands of colored wool together as shown above. Knot both ends.

4 Ask a friend to help you put on the *tunica.* Push the pins through the folded fabric at the shoulders. Tie the belt at the waist and over the flaps of material.

MAKE A PAIR OF ROMAN SANDALS

You will need: brown felt or a square piece of leather, laces, pen, paper, scissors

1 If possible, enlarge the design shown above on a photocopier to fit your foot. Or copy the design onto paper.

2 Cut out the design and draw around it on the fabric.

3 Turn the paper over and copy the design again, for your other foot. Then cut out both shapes.

4 Stand on the center of each piece of fabric. Use laces, or strips of spare fabric, to lace up the loops in the sandal, as shown above.

PURPLE DYE was specially valued by the Romans. It came from a sea snail called the murex, found in parts of the Mediterranean.

WEAR A TOGA

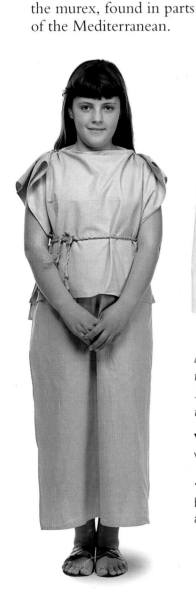

△ *This is a simple way to put on a toga. In reality togas were more difficult to put on.*

You will need: semicircular piece of fabric with a straight edge of 13 ft. (4 m)

1 Hold the straight edge of the fabric behind you. Drape half over your left arm. Tuck this section into your belt.

2 Pass the right half of the *toga* under your right arm and around the front. Tuck a little fold in your belt.

3 Now pass the rest of the fabric over your left shoulder.

Dressing to impress

Wealthy Romans went to great lengths to keep up with changing fashions. They started each day in front of a mirror, attended by slaves who dressed their hair, applied their makeup and perfume, and plucked out unwanted hair with tweezers.

▷ *A wealthy or noble Roman woman spent a lot of time making her hair look beautiful.*

WOMEN'S HAIRSTYLES became more and more elaborate over time. They wore wigs and hairpieces curled with heated tongs and piled up high in rows of curls. Hairpins, made of bone or metal, held the curls in place. Some women wore wigs so that they could change the color of their hair. Blond wigs were made with hair clipped from German slave girls, and black wigs were made with hair imported from India.

MEN WORE LAUREL WREATHS on their heads as a mark of rank. Victorious generals wore them on their return from successful campaigns, and Roman emperors wore them as crowns.

MAKE A LAUREL WREATH

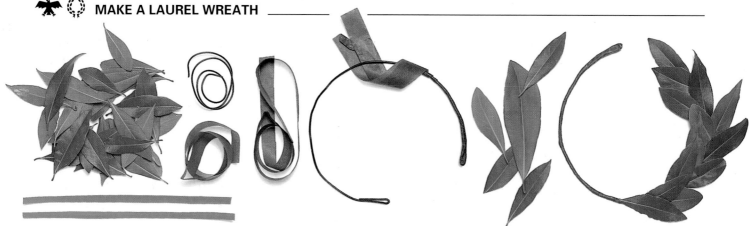

You will need: fresh bay (laurel) leaves or leaves made from green cardboard, strips of green tissue paper, scissors, glue, plastic-coated wire, red ribbon

1 Shape the wire into a headband. Wind and glue strips of tissue paper around the band. Starting at one end, glue the leaves to the tissue paper as shown above right.

2 When you have reached halfway around the headband, start at the other end and glue on the rest of the leaves. Finally, snip the ends of the ribbon in a V-shape, and glue as shown at right.

WEARING MAKEUP was important to noblewomen. They used paint made from chalk and white lead to whiten the face and forearms, and powdered ashes to blacken the eyebrows. Red ocher (from earth), or red wine leftovers were used as rouge for cheeks and lips. Women also used face packs made from damp bread, which they hoped would prevent wrinkles.

◁ *Many women wore beautiful metal bracelets shaped like coiling snakes.*

MAKE A ROMAN BROOCH

You will need: cardboard, glue, safety pin, fine string, tape, paints, paintbrush

1 Draw two flower shapes on the cardboard—one a little larger than the other. Draw four petal shapes, lots of little stamens and a small circle. Cut out the shapes carefully.

2 Glue pieces of string around the petals and the circle. Glue lengths of string to the tips of the stamens.

3 Paint all the cardboard shapes and pieces of string gold.

4 When dry, paint the insides of the petals different colors.

5 Glue the smaller flower on top of the larger one. Bend the edges inward slightly. Glue the stamens onto the center of the flower. Then glue on the petals and the circle as shown.

6 To wear your brooch, tape a safety pin onto the back, as shown above.

▽ *Brooches like these were used to fasten cloaks.*

▽ *The laurel-wreath crown was a symbol of military success and power.*

🌿 ✳ **MEN'S HAIRSTYLES** were influenced by the emperor, whose portrait was engraved on coins (see page 51). Until the A.D. 100'S, men shaved their chins, or had them plucked with tweezers by a barber. This style changed when Emperor Hadrian, who had an ugly scar on his chin, let his beard grow to hide it. Men all over the Empire followed his example.

Some men took just as much trouble over their appearance as women. This is how the historian Suetonius described Emperor Otho: "He was as fussy about his appearance as a woman. His entire body had been plucked of hair and a well-made wig covered his practically bald head… He used a poultice of moist bread to slow down the growth of his beard."

Life in the city

Many Romans lived in the large cities of the Empire. These cities were often built near rivers or close to the sea, because it was much easier to move heavy goods by water than by road. Cities were the main trading centers. There was a constant movement of wagons, pack animals, and merchant ships arriving and departing.

ROMAN CITIES were often built on a grid system. Blocks of buildings called **insulae** were divided by straight streets. Each *insula* was packed with houses, stores, and workshops. To save space, these buildings often joined onto each other, like a row of terraced houses.

▽ *This is a model of a typical Roman town. Most towns and cities had the same key buildings.*

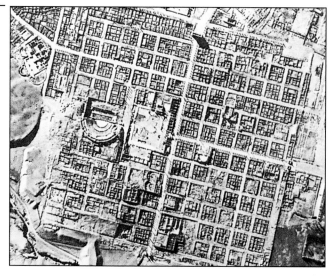

△ *This is an aerial photograph of the Roman town of Timgad in Algeria. The grid system can be seen clearly.*

FRESH WATER was brought into the city by an **aqueduct**. A lot of water was needed for drinking and for the public baths, where Romans went to relax. Many cities also had sewers, and public toilets flushed by water.

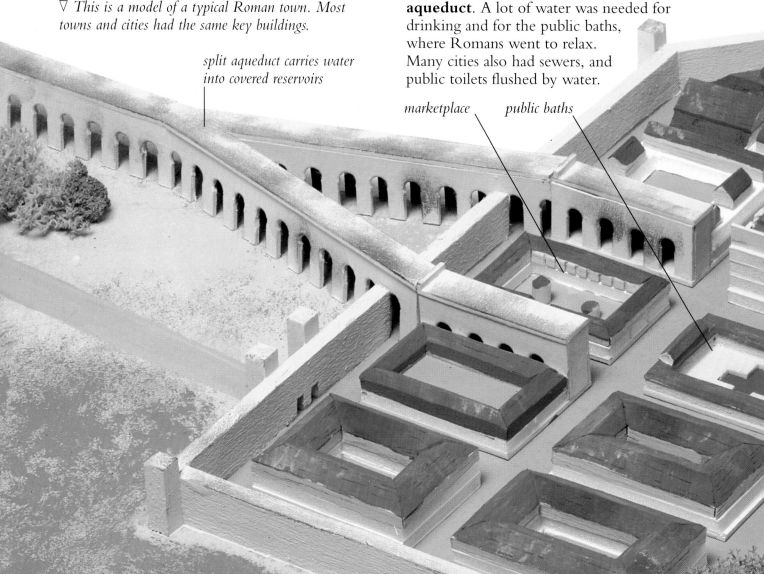

split aqueduct carries water into covered reservoirs

marketplace   public baths

AT THE HEART OF EVERY ROMAN CITY was the **forum**. This was a large open area, used as a market and a public meeting place. Along one side there was a long hall called a *basilica*. This was the law court and the place where merchants and wealthy Romans met to do business.

A smaller building nearby, the *curia*, was where the local council met. The council was responsible for putting on public entertainment, keeping law and order, raising taxes, and looking after the roads, public buildings, and the water supply.

TEMPLES for worshiping the most important gods and the Roman emperor were also built in the forum. Temples to local gods were scattered across the town. Wealthy Romans helped to pay for building temples, and in return had their names carved on them.

PUBLIC ENTERTAINMENT was an important part of city life. There were theaters for plays, and **amphitheaters** where fights between **gladiators** were held (see pages 38–39). Some of the bigger cities even had a racecourse for chariot racing.

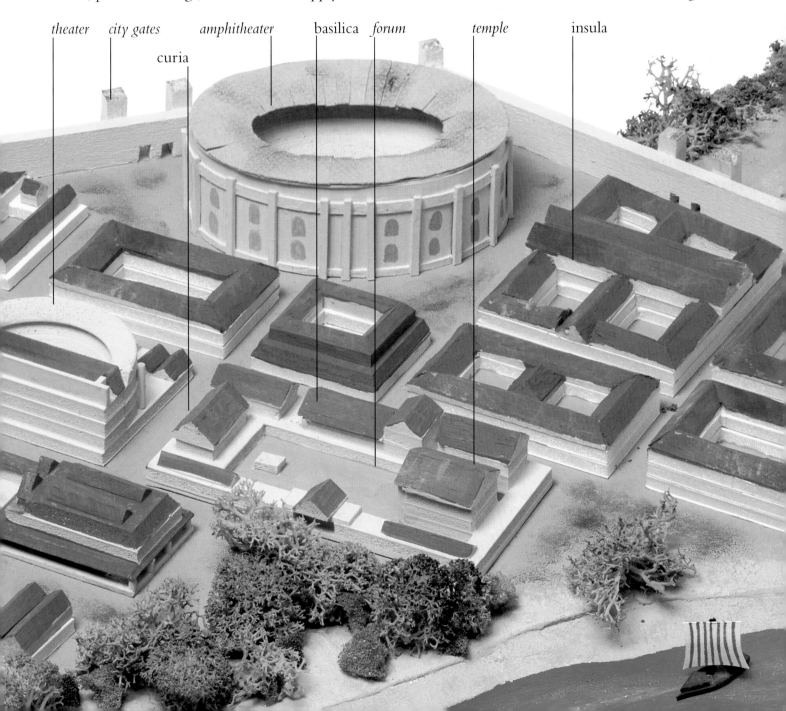

theater   city gates   amphitheater   basilica   *forum*   temple   insula

curia

POMPEII is a town in Italy that was buried under ash when the volcano Vesuvius erupted violently in A.D. 79. Over the past 200 years, the houses and stores of Pompeii have been slowly uncovered. As a result, we have a picture of a whole Roman town as it was on an August day nearly 2,000 years ago.

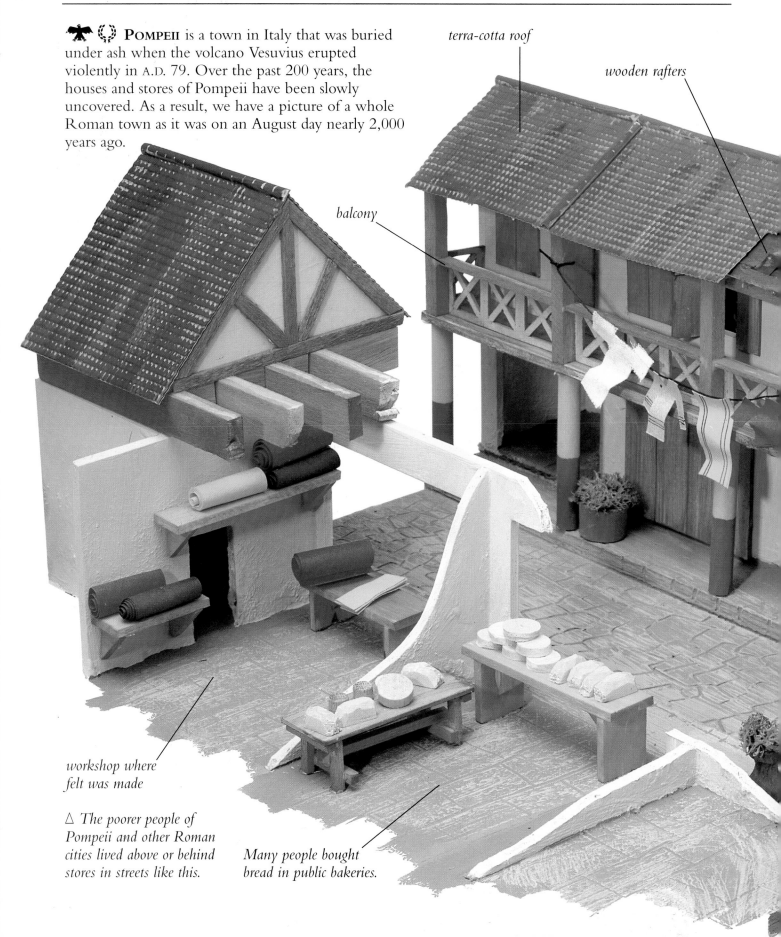

terra-cotta roof

wooden rafters

balcony

workshop where felt was made

△ The poorer people of Pompeii and other Roman cities lived above or behind stores in streets like this.

Many people bought bread in public bakeries.

THE STREETS of Pompeii were lined with a variety of stores and bars. These were often run by freedmen who had their own slaves working for them. Each store had a large open front that was closed up with wooden shutters at night. There was a counter at the front where goods were displayed to customers in the street. Taverns had stone counters with jars set into them for snacks and hot drinks.

△ In this excavated street in Pompeii, you can see the deep ruts in the road made by oxcarts.

THE SIDEWALKS IN POMPEII, like those of many Roman cities, were raised above the level of the road. This prevented oxcarts from knocking over pedestrians. The road sloped slightly so that rainwater and sewage ran into the gutters. Stepping stones were laid across the road to allow people to cross without getting their sandals dirty, and also to slow down the carts.

MOST PEOPLE IN THE EMPIRE were poor, although those who were in charge were very rich. In the larger cities, poor people lived in rented rooms in blocks of apartments. In smaller towns, rich and poor alike lived in the *insulae*, or blocks of housing. A rich family might own a large part of the *insula*, whereas a poor family rented perhaps only one or two rooms.

Inside the homes, furniture was very simple. The poet Martial described a typical room: "There was a little three-legged bed and a two-legged table, with a lamp and a bucket... The neck of an **amphora** held back a little cooker covered in green rust." Most homes did not have bathrooms. Instead, people used chamber pots, which they emptied out of their windows onto the street below.

public drinking fountain

a one-room apartment

tavern

raised sidewalk

gutter

stepping stones

WEALTHY ROMANS lived in very different conditions from the poor. From the outside, the houses of wealthy Romans looked very plain. Because of the risk of burglary, most houses had only a few windows. Rooms were arranged around courtyards and gardens, and openings in the roof let in the maximum amount of light.

△ *In the evenings, homes were lit with pottery lamps. The lamps burned oil made from olives, nuts, or fish.*

THE FIRST ROOM people entered in a Roman house was called the **atrium.** It was a cross between an entrance hall and a courtyard. It had a high ceiling with a skylight in the middle. Below this, in the center of the *atrium*, was an ornamental pool to collect rainwater.

THE DINING ROOM was called a **triclinium,** meaning "three couches." The houses of the rich sometimes had two *triclinia*; a sheltered one for winter, and one with a view of the garden for summer.

THE RECEPTION ROOM was the **tablinum.** This was a cross between a living room and an office where guests were received. Important papers and valuables were kept there, safely locked in a strongbox.

A ROMAN HOUSE was often a crowded place. There were household slaves running errands, children playing with toys, and older women spinning wool (see pages 30–31). There was also a stream of daily visitors or **clients** who came to ask advice and favors from their "patron," who was the head of the house. These were generally people who were less well off. For a wealthy Roman, the day began with a visit from his clients. The more important a Roman was, the greater the number of clients who visited him.

▷ *A wealthy Roman might have lived in a town house like this.*

bedroom
(above tablinum)

peristyle garden (see page 23)

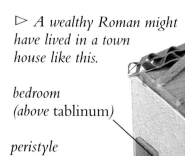

BEDROOMS were often alongside the *atrium*. Apart from the bed, there was little furniture—perhaps a chair and a table, and a pottery chamber pot kept underneath the bed.

CLIENTS were expected to arrive in a clean toga and to call their patron "my lord." They would wait in the *atrium* until they were summoned by a slave to the *tablinum*, where the patron would receive them.

These wealthy patrons were themselves the clients of still richer men. After they had greeted their clients, they might have to visit their own patron. The only man who did not have a patron was the emperor.

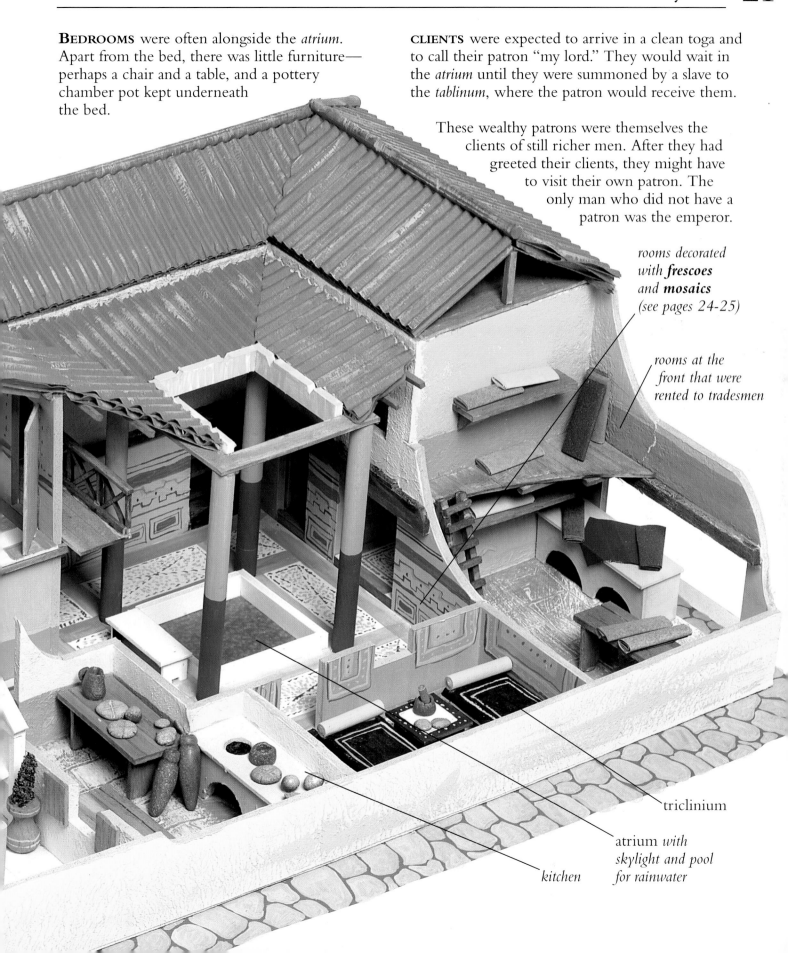

rooms decorated with **frescoes** and **mosaics** (see pages 24-25)

rooms at the front that were rented to tradesmen

triclinium

atrium *with skylight and pool for rainwater*

kitchen

Gardens, mosaics and frescoes _____

Wealthy Romans loved their gardens. They were neatly laid out with rows of clipped hedges and paths, and filled with fountains, pools and statues. A garden was a place to relax on a sunny day, to read or write or just do nothing.

▷ *The gardens of a Roman town house or country villa may have been circular, like this one, or rectangular.*

MANY GARDENS have been discovered at Pompeii. Although the plants there disappeared long ago, their roots have left spaces in the soil. Archaeologists make plaster casts of these spaces to find out what kinds of trees and bushes were planted there.

hedges trimmed to look like birds

lemon tree

small bust of a forest spirit

fountain

FOUNTAINS and ornamental pools were carved from marble. Pliny the Younger, a writer, described the fountains of his garden: "A fountain plays in a marble basin, watering the plane trees round it and the ground beneath them with its light spray… Another has a bowl surrounded by tiny jets which make a lovely murmuring sound."

STATUES of gods and fighting animals were popular garden ornaments. The "House of Stags" in Herculaneum in southern Italy is named after two sculptures of stags being attacked by dogs. There were also statues of forest spirits such as *satyrs*, who were young men with the legs, ears, and horns of goats.

△ Oscilla *were decorated with carvings of gods and satyrs.*

THE PERISTYLE was a type of garden surrounded by roofed columns that provided shade. White marble or terra-cotta disks called *oscilla* were hung between the columns for decoration. They flashed like tiny mirrors as they caught the sun.

SLAVES who were skilled gardeners looked after the garden. They clipped bushes into the shape of animals, birds and gods. The wealthiest Romans also liked to have fish tanks in their gardens, filled with fish, eels and other seafood. They provided a fresh supply for the dinner table! Exotic birds were also popular. Peacocks were imported from India and were thought to be the sacred bird of the goddess Juno.

GARDEN WALLS were sometimes painted with pictures of trees, birds and flowers to make the gardens look bigger. If a house had no real garden, Romans painted garden scenes on a wall, to give the impression of one. Some of these still survive today. They show us what kind of plants the Romans liked to grow.

△ *This mosaic from Pompeii shows a scene from the banks of the Nile River in Egypt. The Romans hunted many of these animals and brought them back to Rome for the games (see pages 38-39).*

THE TOWN HOUSES AND COUNTRY VILLAS of wealthy Romans were full of color. The walls of important rooms, such as the *triclinium* and *tablinum*, were covered with bright paintings called frescoes. The floors were decorated with mosaics—pictures made from thousands of tiny colored tiles and pieces of glass.

MOSAICS were fashionable throughout the Empire. The Romans used the technique, developed by the Greeks, of making black and white patterned floors with pebbles. Later, colored floors became popular. By cutting stones, glass, tiles and shells into little pieces known as *tesserae*, the Romans could make mosaics as detailed as paintings. There were scenes from everyday life, flowers, and different figures such as the gods, gladiators, and actors. One house in Pompeii had a mosaic of a snarling dog in the doorway, with the words *cave canem*—"beware of the dog"—written into the mosaic.

MAKE A MOSAIC

  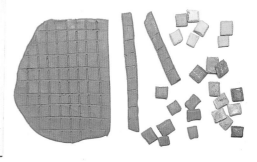

You will need: paper, felt-tip pens, scissors, modeling clay, paints, paintbrush, stiff cardboard, rolling pin, tile adhesive, sponge or stiff brush, varnish (optional)

... fish or another animal. ... a piece of stiff cardboard, ... ough to cover the whole design.

2 Draw your design on a piece of paper and choose the colors you would like to use.

3 Roll out the clay with the rolling pin until it is about ⅛ in. (3 mm) thick.

4 Use a pair of scissors to mark the clay into small squares, as shown above right.

5 Cut the squares to make small tiles, or *tesserae*. Let them dry.

6 Paint them in your chosen colors.

7 To create a more textured effect, you could dip a sponge in the paint and dab it gently onto the tiles. Or you could flick paint onto them, using a stiff brush.

FRESCOES were painted on a freshly plastered wall that was still damp. The color soaked into the plaster and became fixed as it dried. The finished wall was given a protective coat of melted wax mixed with a little oil. Finally, the surface was polished to give it a glossy appearance.

THE FIRST PAINTERS had only a few colors to work with: black from soot, white from chalk, and red and yellow ocher from earth. As the Empire grew, more colors became available. The Egyptians showed the Romans how to make a rich shade of blue from copper. Vermilion, a bright scarlet, came from a mineral called cinnabar that was mined in Spain. Even more exotic and expensive colors were brought by sea from India. You could tell how wealthy Romans were simply by looking at the colors on the walls of their houses.

STYLES OF PAINTING came and went. Until about 80 B.C., walls were painted to look as if they were made of colored marble. Then, architectural scenes with columns and statues became popular. The aim was to make a room look bigger than it really was.

△ *This fresco was discovered on the wall of a town house in Pompeii. The young woman is holding a writing tablet in one hand and a **stylus** in the other (see page 33).*

△ *Mosaics of sea creatures were sometimes used to decorate* triclinium *floors.*

8 Cover the stiff cardboard with a layer of tile adhesive. Press the tiles into the adhesive, following your paper design. Begin with the center tiles and work outward until the design is complete.

9 Let the mosaic dry. You could varnish it later.

Food and feasting

The staple food of most Romans was a type of stew made of wheat, barley, beans, or lentils. However, rich Romans had a more varied diet. They ate food grown on their own farms, and more expensive dishes imported from all over the Empire.

COOKING was a luxury for most people who lived in cities. Because of the risk of fire in their wooden apartments, the poor bought their meals from stalls in the street instead of cooking. Wealthy Romans had their own kitchens and slaves who cooked for them.

food cooked on a raised hearth

amphorae

MAKE A HONEY OMELET

You will need: 5 eggs, ground pepper, ⅓ oz. (10 g) butter, 5 tablesp. (75 ml) milk, 1 teasp. (5 ml) honey, 1 oz. (25 g) almonds, dash of anchovy essence or soy sauce

1 Whisk the eggs in a bowl. Then add the honey, pepper, and milk.

2 Ask an adult to put the almonds on a baking tray and bake them in a hot oven at 325° F (165° C) for 20 min.

3 When cool, ask an adult to chop the nuts with a sharp knife. Now add them to the egg mixture.

4 Stir the anchovy essence or soy sauce into the egg mixture.

5 Melt the butter in a frying pan and pour in the egg mixture. Cook until the omelet is firm, turning once.

BRICK OVENS were used for baking and roasting. A fire was lit inside, heating the bricks. When the fire died, the ashes were raked out and bread or meat was put in the oven. The entrance was covered and food cooked by the heat of the bricks.

◁ *A wealthy Roman had a kitchen like this one.*

flour

bowl for grinding spices

POTTERY JARS, or *amphorae*, leaned against the kitchen walls. They held the most commonly used ingredients—olive oil, vinegar, wine, and fish sauce.

THE MOST POPULAR FOOD FLAVORING was a spicy fish sauce called *garum*. It was made from the blood and internal parts of mackerel, an oily type of fish. The fish parts were salted, mixed with vinegar and herbs, and left in the sun until they turned into liquid. *Garum* had a powerful flavor. Only a tiny amount was needed to flavor a dish.

THE ROMANS COOKED in ways rather different from how we cook today. They used honey to sweeten food, because they did not have sugar. They also loved pepper, which came from India. They even sprinkled it on desserts and mixed it with wine.

MAKE GRAPE PUNCH

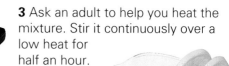

3 Ask an adult to help you heat the mixture. Stir it continuously over a low heat for half an hour.

4 Let cool before serving.

You will need: 4 tablesp. of honey, crushed bay leaf, 2 dates, 1 qt. (1 l) white grape juice, pinch of cinnamon, ground pepper, saffron, and lemon for flavor and decoration

1 Chop the dates fine. Discard the pits.

2 Place all the ingredients in a saucepan.

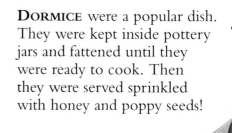

ENTERTAINING generally took place in the evening, when wealthy Romans invited guests to dinner. They ate in the *triclinium*, or dining room, stretched out on three couches.

◁ *The Romans made beautiful glassware, which they used when they entertained.*

EACH COUCH could seat three people, so the perfect number of guests at a dinner party was nine. The couches were arranged to make three sides of a square, with the fourth side left open for the slaves who brought the dishes.

▷ *The Romans served this spiced punch cold before a meal, or warm during a meal.*

DORMICE were a popular dish. They were kept inside pottery jars and fattened until they were ready to cook. Then they were served sprinkled with honey and poppy seeds!

mosaics of food scraps

THE PLACE OF HONOR was on the right-hand side of the host, who was in the center of the middle couch. The guests propped themselves up on their elbows and ate with their fingers. Between courses they washed their hands in finger bowls and dried them with napkins. Guests often brought their own napkins, so that they could take away any of the delicious food they had been unable to finish.

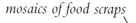

ROMANS SHOWED OFF THEIR WEALTH by serving food brought from all the corners of the Empire. Certain provinces were famous for particular delicacies. Libya, for example, was the place to find truffles, while Syria was known for its delicious pears.

burning lamps for light

▽ *A Roman dinner party in the* triclinium.

UNUSUAL DISHES were especially impressive. The Emperor Vitellius, famous for his love of food, served some of the most expensive meals in history. One of his dishes, called "Shield of Minerva," was described by the historian Suetonius: "The recipe called for pike-livers, pheasant-brains, peacock-brains, flamingo-tongues, and lamprey-eggs [an eel-like fish]; and the ingredients, collected in every corner of the Empire… were brought to Rome in naval *triremes* [warships]."

THROUGHOUT THE MEAL, slaves who were musicians, storytellers, and jugglers would entertain the guests. The type of entertainment depended on the tastes of the host. He might want to read legal speeches or extracts from his poetry. Another host might only be interested in belly-dancing!

Family life

The word *family* is Roman and comes from the Latin word *familia*. In Roman times, a family meant the household, which included slaves, freedmen, and freedwomen.

POORER ROMANS were rarely educated. Unlike the wealthy, they did not write books and could not afford carved tombstones for their graves. Most of what we know about the daily lives of Romans comes from these sources. Because the rich were generally interested only in their own lives, not much is known about poorer Romans.

▷ *Young children played with terra-cotta rattles shaped like animals. This jewel-studded pig probably belonged to a child with wealthy parents.*

charm, or bulla—*a young boy's pendant*

family shrine

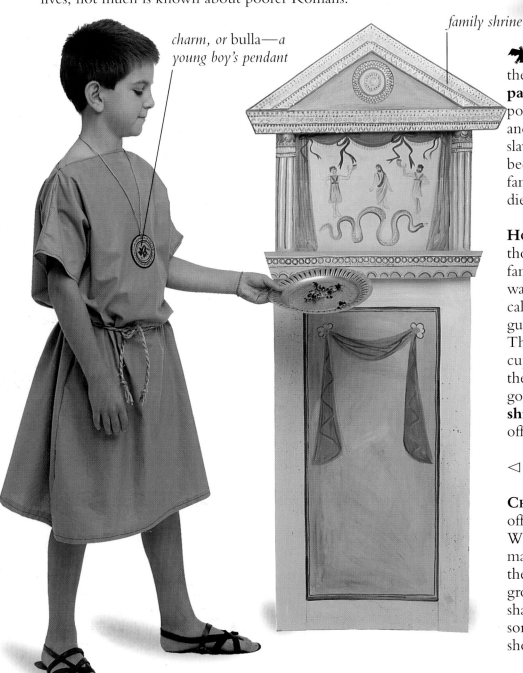

THE FAMILY HEAD was the father. He was known as the **pater familias.** He had total power over all family members and had the right to sell them into slavery, or even to kill them. Sons became the *pater familias* of their families only when their fathers died.

HOUSEHOLD GODS were thought to watch over every family. The head of the house was protected by a guardian spirit called his *Genius*, while his wife's guardian spirit was called her *Juno*. The *Penates* looked after the food cupboards, and the *Lares* protected the home. Small statues of these gods were kept in a household **shrine** and the family made offerings to them.

◁ *A boy offers a tuft of hair to the gods.*

CHILDREN made their own offerings to the household gods. When girls became engaged to be married, they left their toy dolls at the shrine as a sign that they were grown up. When boys were first shaved by the barber, they offered some of the hair to the gods to show that they had become men.

MAKE A ROMAN TOY DOLL

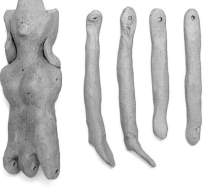

You will need: modeling clay, needle, string, paints, paintbrush

1 Model the clay into the parts of a doll: two arms, two legs, a body and head, as shown above right. At the base of the body, make two indents for the legs.

2 With the needle, make holes in the top of the arms and legs, through the base of the body, and right through the chest. The holes must be large enough for the string to be threaded through.

3 Let the clay parts dry.

4 Paint your doll as shown. Add a pattern around the neck, waist, and hair for decoration. Let it dry.

5 Thread string through the holes in the chest and arms. Knot the ends. Do the same with the legs.

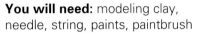

▷ *Roman children played with spinning tops, carved wooden animals, hoops, and dolls like this one.*

🦅 ⚜ MARRIAGE

had a dramatic effect on the lives of Roman women. In early times, when a young girl married, she had to leave her own *familia* and join her husband's. This meant that she had to live by the rules of a new *pater familias*. But by the end of the Republic, the Romans had invented a new system of marriage in which a wife legally remained part of her own *familia*. This gave her more freedom. She kept control of her own property and if her husband divorced her, he had to return her possessions to her.

DIVORCE was common, especially among wealthy Romans. A husband could divorce his wife if the marriage was childless, or if he wanted to marry someone else. But wives did not have the right to divorce their husbands.

WIVES were responsible for running the household, giving orders to slaves and looking after the children. They also spent a lot of time spinning thread from wool to make clothes. In marriage ceremonies, a bride often carried a spindle for hand-spinning as a symbol of her duties as a wife.

Education and trades

Life for the sons and daughters of wealthy Romans was very different from the lives of poor children. Children of the wealthy were educated at home or at school, while poorer children went out to learn a trade.

POOR CHILDREN did not go to school. From an early age, they were expected to help their parents at work. A young boy aged eight or nine would either follow in his father's footsteps or work as an apprentice in the trade of a family friend. To begin with, child workers were usually given the most unpleasant tasks, but by watching and helping, boys learned the skills of blacksmiths, bakers, launderers and goldsmiths. Girls stayed with their mothers and helped in the store, the workshop, or the kitchen.

▷ *This is a Roman inkpot and pen from the first century* A.D.

RICH CHILDREN began their education at home, where they were taught by a well-educated slave called a *pedagogue*. At the age of 11, some boys and girls went to a school run by a *grammaticus*, or grammar teacher, to study literature. They learned to speak Greek and memorized Greek and Latin poetry, taking turns to recite it. Roman noblemen and women loved quoting poetry in their conversations and letters.

PUBLIC SPEAKING was considered to be essential for all young men wishing to become politicians or lawyers. A tutor called a *rhetor* taught pupils how to present an opinion in a logical way and how to speak persuasively. Pupils practiced these skills by imagining they were taking part in law cases, either defending or accusing.

◁ *In Pompeii, young boys were employed in laundries to clean cloth in large vats by treading it with their feet.*

MAKE A WRITING TABLET

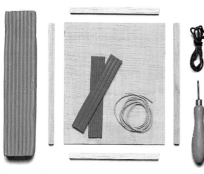

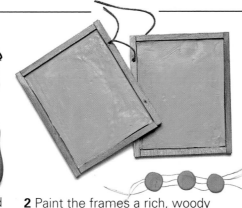

You will need: balsa wood, red and green modeling clay, craft knife, ruler, glue, string, paint, awl, stick

1 For both frames cut a flat piece of wood 7 x 5½ in. (18 x 14 cm), four thick strips of wood: two measuring 7 x ⅓ in. (18 x 1 cm), and two measuring 5½ x ⅓ in. (14 x 1 cm). Glue together as shown above right.

2 Paint the frames a rich, woody color. With the bradawl, make two holes in one side of each frame. Thread string through the holes and tie the frames together.

3 Make seals to decorate. Cut three 8-in. (20-cm) lengths of string. Press the string into three red clay disks. Glue to the back of the tablet.

4 Roll out two flat pieces of green clay and glue inside each frame as shown.

5 To make a *stylus*, ask an adult to help you sharpen the end of a stick. Use it to write on the tablet. Smooth over the clay to use again.

ROMAN NUMERALS

1	I	7	VII	40	XL
2	II	8	VIII	50	L
3	III	9	IX	60	LX
4	IV	10	X	90	XC
5	V	20	XX	100	C
6	VI	30	XXX	500	D
				1,000	M

ROMANS used letters to represent numbers, and they are still used today on many clocks and watches. Each letter has a different value and can be combined with other letters to make bigger numbers. I is used for 1, X for 10, C for 100, and M for 1,000. For example, 1,326 is shown as MCCCXXVI. This made it quite tricky to do calculations with large numbers, especially multiplication and long division.

PUPILS wrote on thin sheets of wood using pens made of reeds or brass. They also wrote on beeswax tablets using a pen called a *stylus* to scratch letters onto the tablet. One end of the *stylus* was flat, so that the wax could be smoothed over and reused.

IN SOME ROMAN TOWNS walls were covered with advertisements, so it is likely that many of the poor could read. Despite the lack of formal teaching, many poorer Romans learned to read and write a little—enough to sign their name and write a few simple documents.

▷ *A noblewoman reads a letter written on a wax writing tablet.*

Gods of the Empire

The Romans believed in many gods and goddesses who were thought to watch over different aspects of their lives. From very early times the Romans adopted Greek myths, linking the legends of the Greek gods with their own. They told the same stories about Jupiter that the Greeks told of their god, Zeus.

THE MOST IMPORTANT GODS were Jupiter, ruler of gods and men, and king of heaven; his wife Juno, queen of heaven and goddess of women and marriage; and Jupiter's daughter Minerva, goddess of wisdom and art. Together, they shared the Temple of Jupiter Capitolinus in Rome. Temples were places to worship the gods. They were also places to leave valuables for safekeeping, like banks today. It was thought that thieves would not dare to rob the house of a god.

▽ *Musicians herald the arrival of the procession.*

long, curved horn called a cornu

double pipes

▽ *The* victimarius *(sacrificing priest) carries an ax.*

a sheep is led to the altar as an offering to the gods

RELIGIOUS CEREMONIES were conducted by a priest or priestess in front of the temple building. Processions of people brought gifts as offerings to a particular god. In return they hoped to win the god's favor. Bulls, sheep, and pigs were decorated with flowers and led to the temple. The priest or priestess sacrificed the animal on an altar in front of the temple, and then burned some of the meat. The rising smoke was supposed to carry the offering up to the god.

PREDICTING THE FUTURE was an important part of religion. The Romans believed that the gods sent messages to warn of coming disasters, or as a sign of good luck. There were different ways of reading these messages. **Augurs** were priests who told the future by studying birds. **Haruspices** were men who examined the inner organs of a sacrificed animal to find out if the god had accepted the offering.

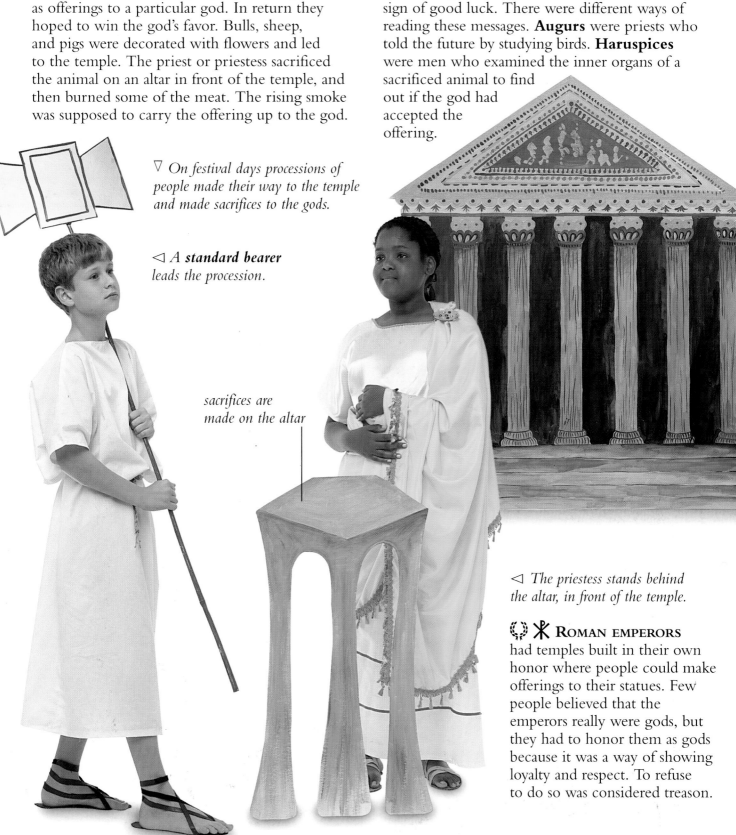

▽ *On festival days processions of people made their way to the temple and made sacrifices to the gods.*

◁ *A* **standard bearer** *leads the procession.*

sacrifices are made on the altar

◁ *The priestess stands behind the altar, in front of the temple.*

ROMAN EMPERORS had temples built in their own honor where people could make offerings to their statues. Few people believed that the emperors really were gods, but they had to honor them as gods because it was a way of showing loyalty and respect. To refuse to do so was considered treason.

△ *This statue depicts Mithras slaying a mythical bull. The bull's blood was believed to be the source of all life.*

○ **AS THE EMPIRE EXPANDED,** the Romans came into contact with people who worshiped different gods. Some of these foreign gods were just like their own. Other gods, like **Mithras** and Isis, seemed very different, partly because they offered the promise of life after death.

○ **THE CULTS OF MITHRAS AND ISIS** were spread throughout the Empire by merchants, traders, soldiers, and slaves. These gods were worshiped at secret ceremonies, unlike Roman gods who were worshiped in public. Mithras was the god of light from Persia (ancient Iran). He was worshiped by men who met by torchlight in underground rooms.

Isis was an Egyptian mother goddess and the special protector of seafarers. Followers of Isis were persecuted until the Emperor Caligula allowed people to worship Isis and built a temple to her.

MAKE A VOTIVE OFFERING

You will need: thin cardboard, strips of newspaper, flour, water, salt, wire, large needle, ribbon, bronze paint, paintbrush

1 Draw a leg or hand and a candy shape on cardboard as shown, then cut them out.

2 Make a paste from flour and water. Add a pinch of salt. Cover the cardboard with a few layers of newspaper strips dipped in the paste. Let dry.

3 Paint the cardboard shapes bronze.

4 You could write your name in Roman capital letters with a needle as shown at right.

5 Coil pieces of wire into rings. Make a hole at the top and bottom of the candy shape and thread the rings through.

6 Make a hole in the leg or arm shape and attach it to the bottom ring. Tie the ribbon to the top ring.

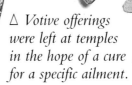

△ *Votive offerings were left at temples in the hope of a cure for a specific ailment.*

◯ **VOTIVES,** or dedicated offerings, were used in temples throughout the Empire. Romans believed that the gods had the power to cause and cure illness, so people who were sick went to the temple to pray. As offerings to the gods, they left a small model that showed the part of the body that needed healing, with a few words inscribed on it.

◯ **SOME RELIGIOUS PRACTICES** are shrouded in mystery. Face pots, some containing ashes of the dead, have been found at Roman sites in Britain and Germany. They were discovered in graves, under buildings, and in streams. No one knows what the faces mean: they may represent a dead person, a god, or a mask.

◯ ✳ **MAKE A FACE POT**

You will need: modeling clay, poster paints, paintbrush

1 Roll the clay into several long sausage shapes. Coil a length of clay into a round base shape as shown above.

2 Carefully add another coil of clay and build up your pot in this way. Use your thumbs to smooth the outside of the pot and merge the coils.

3 Make little clay petal shapes for the rim of the pot. Then make a mouth, eyes, eyebrows, nose and ears.

4 Add the petal shapes and facial features. Smooth the pot at the joined places. Let it dry. Paint it brown.

◯ **CHRISTIANITY** spread from Palestine in the Eastern Empire during the first century A.D. Like Mithras and Isis, Christ was seen as a god who promised eternal life. Unlike those gods however, his religion was open to everyone, including slaves and the poor. At first, Rome's rulers tried to stamp out this new religion because Christians refused to pay respect to the Roman gods, or worship the emperor.

✳ **ATTITUDES TO CHRISTIANITY CHANGED** when the Emperor Constantine came to power. He became a Christian, and in A.D. 313 he gave Christians the freedom of worship and encouraged Romans to convert.

△ *Face pots, or funerary urns, were used in burial rituals.*

At the games

The Romans had very bloodthirsty tastes in entertainment. They loved watching people and animals killing each other in the amphitheater. There were many amphitheaters in the Empire, but the greatest was the Colosseum in Rome.

THE COLOSSEUM in Rome opened in A.D. 80 and held up to 50,000 people. The games usually began with bloody battles between wild animals. Then the gladiatorial contests followed. To celebrate the opening of the arena, 5,000 animals were slaughtered in the arena on the first day.

▽ *The Colosseum in Rome.*

△ *Romans hunting animals in North Africa for the games*

DURING THE FIRST HALF OF THE GAMES, wild animals, such as rhinoceroses, lions, elephants, and bulls were pitted against gladiators, and each other, or let loose on criminals.

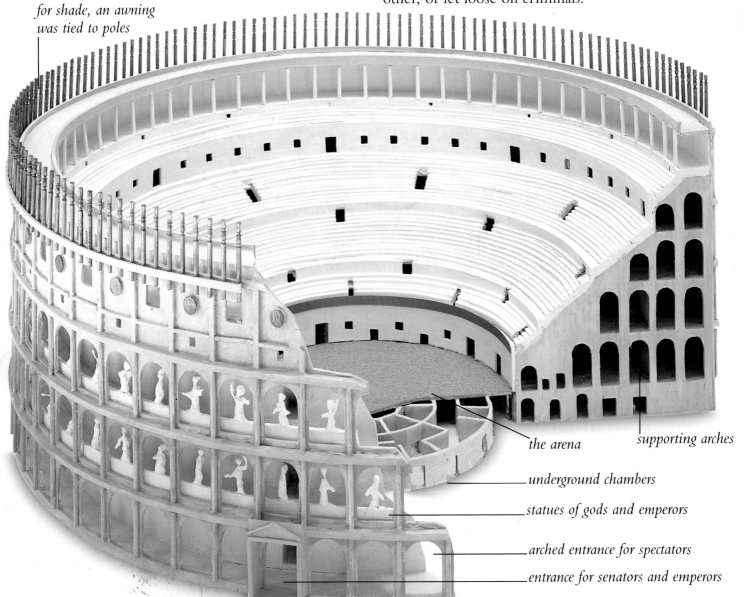

for shade, an awning was tied to poles

the arena

supporting arches

underground chambers

statues of gods and emperors

arched entrance for spectators

entrance for senators and emperors

GLADIATORS were usually slaves or criminals, although some freedmen also earned their living this way. A gladiator's life was short and hard; the majority survived only a few fights.

SUCCESSFUL GLADIATORS were treated rather like the film stars of today. They were well-trained champions who were taught combat techniques at special schools. There were different types of gladiators: the *retiarius* was armed as a fisherman, with a net and a trident—he was often pitted against a *murmillo*, the fishman. Each type of gladiator had its own group of devoted fans.

A CONTEST LASTED until one gladiator was killed or badly wounded. The wounded man threw away his weapons and begged for mercy. The crowd would shout a verdict. If the gladiator had fought well, the emperor would give a "thumbs-up" sign and spare his life. If he had not fought well, the emperor gave the "thumbs-down" sign. Then the victorious gladiator would kill the loser. An attendant dressed as a demon clubbed the loser on the head and dragged his body out through the "gate of death."

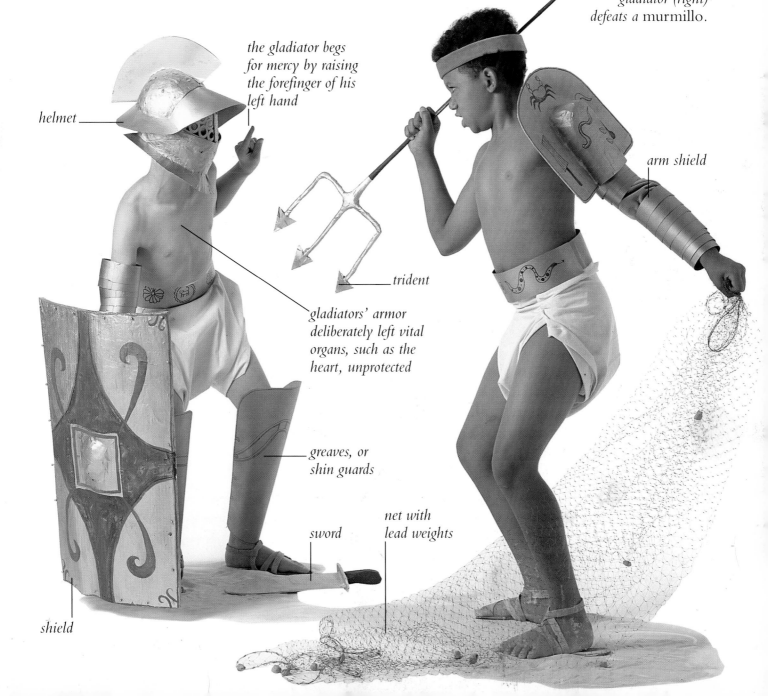

▽ *A* retiarius *gladiator (right) defeats a* murmillo.

the gladiator begs for mercy by raising the forefinger of his left hand

helmet

arm shield

trident

gladiators' armor deliberately left vital organs, such as the heart, unprotected

greaves, or shin guards

net with lead weights

sword

shield

CHARIOT RACING was the most popular entertainment in the larger cities of the Empire. The Romans may have taken the sport from the Greeks, who had been racing horses for over a thousand years.

RACES TOOK PLACE on a long track called a **circus**. The biggest of all, Rome's Circus Maximus, could hold 250,000 spectators. The circus was a place to meet friends, to gamble on the horses, and to enjoy a dangerous and spectacular show.

▷ *Chariots were made of lightweight pieces of wood, lashed together with thongs. This bronze statue once depicted a two-horse chariot.*

▽ *Watching chariot racing at the Circus Maximus in Rome was a favorite pastime for many Romans.*

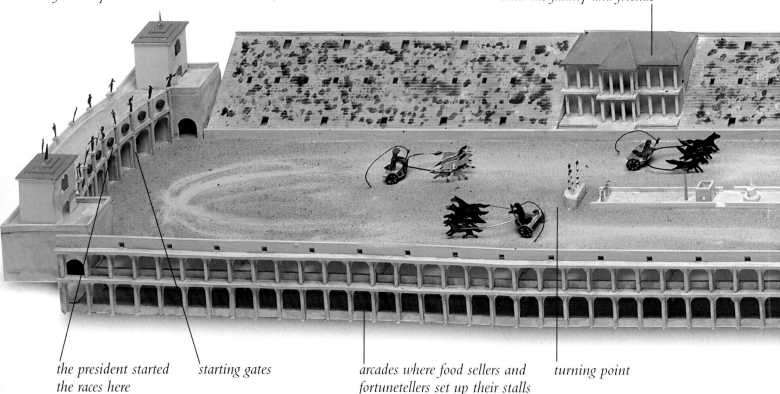

the emperor sat in the imperial box with his family and friends

the president started the races here

starting gates

arcades where food sellers and fortunetellers set up their stalls

turning point

THERE WERE FOUR TEAMS—the Whites, Reds, Blues, and the Greens. Each team had its own horses, riders and stables, staffed with trainers, veterinarians, and slaves. Like football fans of today, racegoers supported one particular team. They gambled money on their team and wore its colors. The Blues and the Greens had the most supporters. Their rival fans hated each other so much that the races sometimes ended in riots.

THE RACE TRACK was the only public place where men and women could sit together. According to the poet Ovid, the circus was a good place to find a girlfriend: "Sit as close as you like; no one will stop you at all. In fact, you have to sit close—that's one of the rules at the race track... Ask her, 'Whose colors are those?'—that's good for an opening. Put your bet down, fast, on whatever she plays... Girls, as everyone knows, adore these little attentions."

THE PRESIDENT OF THE RACES sat at one end of the circus, and it was his responsibility to get the race underway. At the blast of a trumpet, he stood up and held out a white napkin, which he dropped onto the track. At this signal, the starting gates flew open and the chariots came racing out.

The starting gates were situated at one end of the circus. Two or four chariots raced seven times around a long, narrow structure called a *spina* that had turning points at each end. The race finished opposite the judges' boxes about halfway along one side.

THE MOST DANGEROUS MOMENT was turning the chariots at the end of the track. If they were too close to the turning posts, they might crash into each other, or overturn. If they were too far away, the charioteers could lose their position.

CHARIOTEERS were mostly slaves. If they won races they could buy their freedom and grow very rich. The teams paid their stars huge salaries to stop them from joining a rival team. The fans admired their skill and courage so much that they kept busts and portraits of the charioteers in their homes. However, many charioteers died young, crushed under the hooves of the galloping horses.

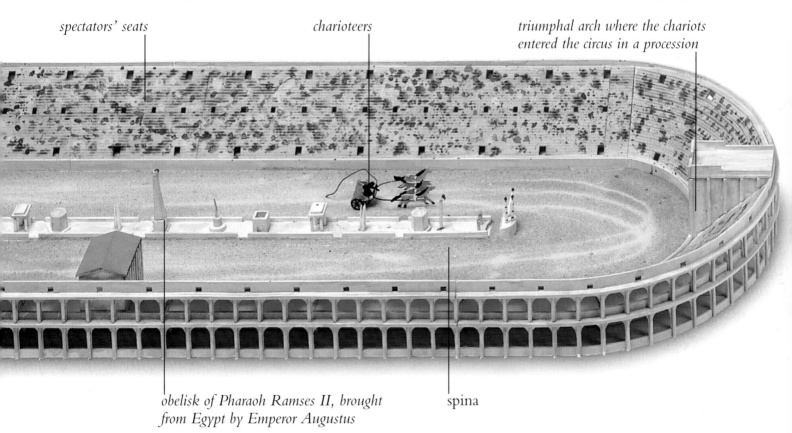

spectators' seats

charioteers

triumphal arch where the chariots entered the circus in a procession

obelisk of Pharaoh Ramses II, brought from Egypt by Emperor Augustus

spina

THE CENTRAL "BACKBONE," or *spina*, of the circus, was decorated with statues of the gods and goddesses who were thought to watch over sport. There were also seven large wooden eggs and seven bronze dolphins on the *spina*. At the end of every lap, an egg was removed and a dolphin was reversed to show how many laps remained. Each end of the *spina* was marked by three tall posts.

THE BEST HORSES were also treated like stars. The Emperor Caligula had a favorite horse called *Incitatus* (Speedy) that raced for the Greens. He went to great lengths to keep his horse happy. On the day before a race, troops surrounded the stable, making sure that no one made any loud noises that might disturb *Incitatus*. Caligula even gave the horse a house complete with furniture and slaves!

Romans relaxing

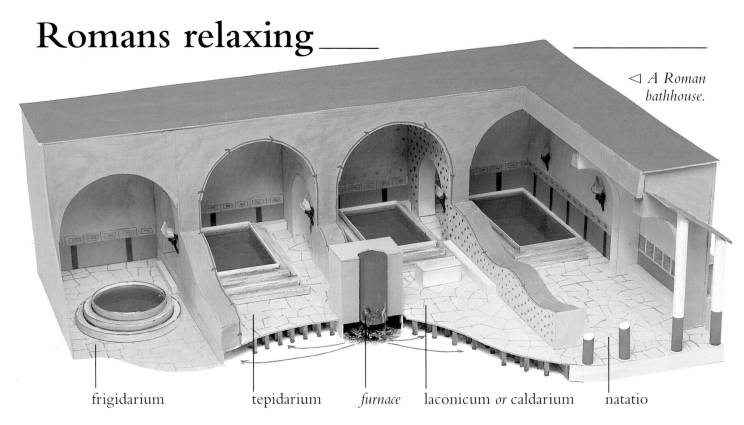

△ *A Roman bathhouse.*

frigidarium   tepidarium   *furnace*   laconicum *or* caldarium   natatio

Every Roman town had at least one large public bathhouse. This was a place where people could go to wash the dust off, to exercise, or just to relax. Men and women visited the bathhouse separately, either at different times or in different areas. It cost very little to go to the baths, so only the poorest people could not afford to visit them. Many Romans went every day.

▷ *Oils were kept in the small pot, and the long, curved **strigil** was used for scraping off the oil and dirt.*

THE BATHHOUSE had a large exercise yard where people played ball games, lifted weights, and wrestled. After exercising, they went to a series of heated rooms to wash and relax.

THE ROOMS and bathwater were heated by a furnace stoked by slaves. Hot air from the fire passed through spaces under the floors and inside the walls. The hottest room was the one closest to the furnace.

Once inside, the bathers first went to an icy plunge pool called a *frigidarium*. From there they passed to a warmer room—the *tepidarium*. This was where oils were applied to the skin and then scraped off, so that the bather would be thoroughly clean.

INSTEAD OF SOAP, Romans used olive oil. They rubbed it all over their bodies and scraped it off with a curved metal tool called a *strigil*. Wealthy Romans had personal slave attendants to scrape them down. Poorer Romans had to rub their backs against the walls to scrape the parts they couldn't reach!

FINALLY, THE BATHERS went to a steam room, called a *caldarium*, or to the *laconicum*, or hot room. Then they were clean enough to swim in the swimming pool, or *natatio*. Around the pool there were entertainers, hairdressers and people selling food and drink. Businessmen even held meetings at the baths.

KNUCKLEBONES, or *astragali,* was a popular game at the baths. Players used the small anklebones of a sheep, which have six sides. It was an easy game to play: a player would throw the bones up into the air and try to catch them on the back of the hand. Knucklebones could also be played like dice, with each side of the bones having a different value. Wealthy Romans played with knucklebones made of marble, silver, or precious stones.

MAKE KNUCKLEBONES

You will need: modeling clay, poster paints, paintbrush

1 Mold the clay into 10 knucklebone shapes with 6 sides as shown above.

▽ *Roman girls and women loved to relax at the baths by playing knucklebones.*

2 Paint the knucklebones and give five to each player.

The basic way to play knucklebones is described on the left. Each player should throw in turn. Try and catch as many bones on the back of your hand as possible. Keep count of the number you manage to catch.

△ *This mosaic from Pompeii shows actors and musicians getting ready for a performance.*

THEATER was invented by the Greeks. The Romans borrowed two main types of plays from them: the first was tragedy, a serious play showing the sufferings of a great hero or heroine, usually from a Greek myth. The second was comedy, a light-hearted play about everyday life. Many Roman plays were set in Greece and performed by Greek actors.

AUDIENCES were often very noisy. People either cheered the actors or shouted insults at them. The producer of *The Mother-in-Law*, a comedy by Terence, described his lively audience: "I was successful in holding the audience— at least to the end of the first act. But then a rumor spread that some gladiators were going to perform—and my audience flew off in a huge crowd, pushing, shouting, fighting to get a good spot at the gladiator performance."

MASKS were worn in most types of play. These larger-than-life masks showed the sex of the character, as well as his or her mood. Thanks to the masks, the audience could tell at once if an actor was meant to be an angry old man, a comical slave, or a beautiful woman. Masks for tragedy showed an expression of horror or despair.

PANTOMIME was a performance in which a single actor mimed several parts, using a series of masks with closed mouths. It was like a solo ballet dance and demanded a great deal of skill. With their faces covered, the actors relied on movement to show their feelings. Pantomime actors were the big stars of the Roman stage.

▽ *This is a mask that an actor might have worn in a tragic play.*

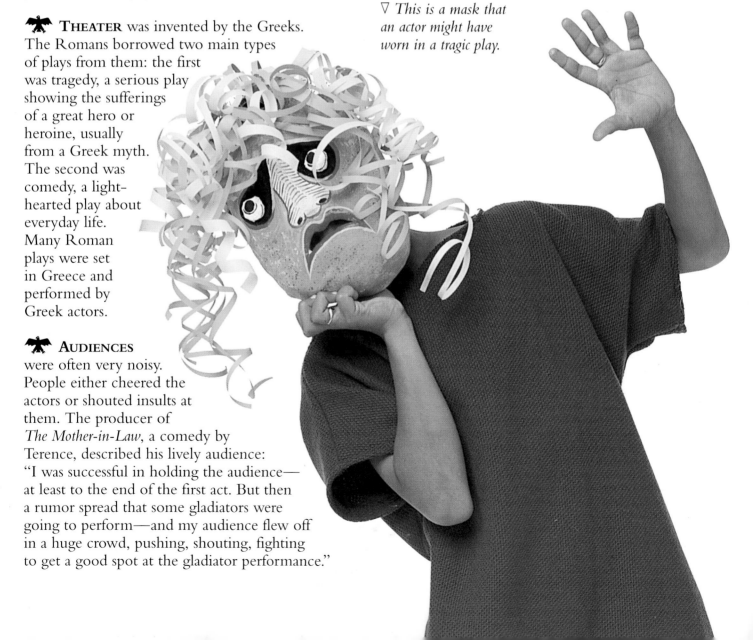

3 Paint your drum as shown above.

4 Make four tassels with your yarn and glue them around your drum.

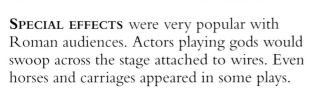

You will need: two lengths of cardboard measuring 2⅓ x 35 in. (6 x 90 cm), paint, paintbrush, yarn, glue, double-sided adhesive tape, a circle of fabric 12½ in. (32 cm) in diameter

1 Glue the ends of one of the pieces of cardboard together to make a circle. Stretch the fabric over the circle and glue down tightly around the edges to make the drum.

2 Stick a strip of adhesive tape along the other length of cardboard. Wrap around the drum.

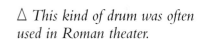

SPECIAL EFFECTS were very popular with Roman audiences. Actors playing gods would swoop across the stage attached to wires. Even horses and carriages appeared in some plays.

△ *This kind of drum was often used in Roman theater.*

MUSIC was very important in the theater. Musicians played the pipes, trumpets, cymbals, and drums, while the actors sang songs. Although we know what instruments were played, we have no way of knowing what Roman music sounded like.

◁ *This actor is wearing a comic mask. Actors used masks and hand gestures to show different characters.*

Amazing architects

The Romans were among the best builders in history. They built things that served practical purposes, such as canals, bridges, sewers, harbors, and roads. But it was perhaps in constructing aqueducts that their engineering skills were most impressive.

▽ *Rome was served by eight aqueducts, each built using wooden scaffolding such as this.*

△ *This Roman aqueduct still stands in Segovia, in central Spain.*

covered water channel

AQUEDUCTS were developed by the Romans. They are channels for carrying water that were mostly dug into the earth, following the contours of hills. Where this was not possible, the Romans built arches made of concrete and stone. It took great skill to build an aqueduct. The water channel had to slope at exactly the right angle all the way along its length to give a steady flow of water.

AN ARCH is a curved structure that is able to support great weight. By using arches, the Romans found they could build high, strong walls using as little stone as possible.

CONCRETE was also a Roman invention. It was a mixture of volcanic sand and stone rubble, held together by mortar made from lime and water. It was strong, cheap, and much easier to use than stone blocks. Concrete and arches made it possible to build structures like the Colosseum.

PLINY THE ELDER described the work involved in giving Rome its water supply: "If we think of the abundant supply of water for public buildings, baths, settling tanks, pools, private houses, gardens, and country estates close to the city; and of the distance the water travels, the height of the arches, the tunneling through mountains, the leveling of routes across deep valleys; we can only conclude that this is a supreme wonder of the world."

▷ *This surveyor is using a* groma—*a wooden cross mounted on a pole, with weighted strings at the ends that hung vertically.*

wooden scaffolding supports arches as they are being built

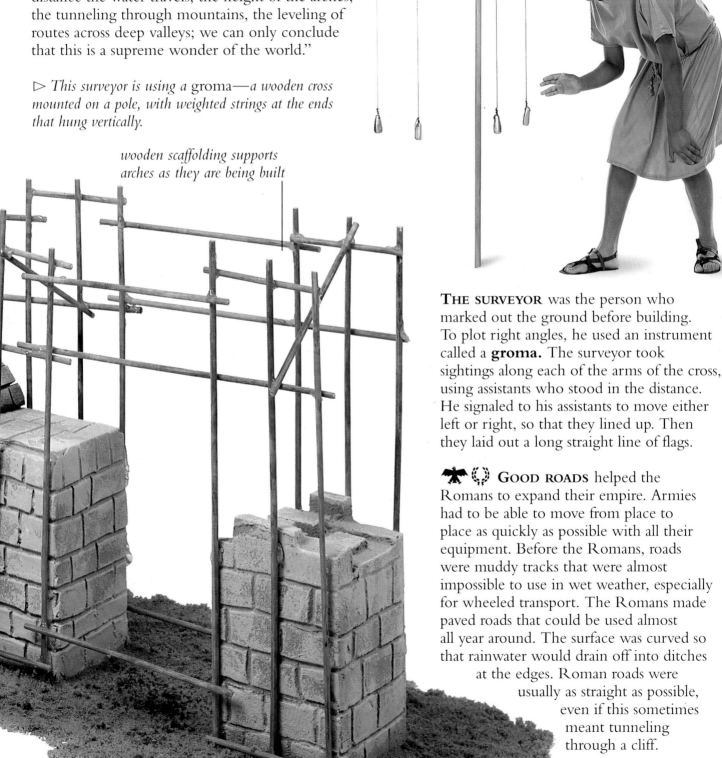

THE SURVEYOR was the person who marked out the ground before building. To plot right angles, he used an instrument called a **groma.** The surveyor took sightings along each of the arms of the cross, using assistants who stood in the distance. He signaled to his assistants to move either left or right, so that they lined up. Then they laid out a long straight line of flags.

GOOD ROADS helped the Romans to expand their empire. Armies had to be able to move from place to place as quickly as possible with all their equipment. Before the Romans, roads were muddy tracks that were almost impossible to use in wet weather, especially for wheeled transport. The Romans made paved roads that could be used almost all year around. The surface was curved so that rainwater would drain off into ditches at the edges. Roman roads were usually as straight as possible, even if this sometimes meant tunneling through a cliff.

Feeding the Empire

Some of the best farmland in the Roman Empire was along the coast of North Africa. The soil there was good and the climate was excellent, with long, hot summers and regular rain in winter. It was the perfect place for growing wheat—in fact, North Africa produced two-thirds of the grain eaten in Rome.

△ *This mosaic from the A.D. 300's shows farm laborers gathering and treading grapes.*

ROMAN FARMS were often enormous and were owned by very wealthy people. In the first century A.D., half of North Africa was said to belong to just six men. Roman landlords spent most of their time in the cities, living extravagantly. They either rented the land out to tenants, or left their farms in the hands of a bailiff who was in charge of a gang of slaves.

FARM BUILDINGS included barns for storing grain and straw, stables for the animals, and various workshops—a blacksmith's forge for making and repairing tools, and a pottery for making storage jars. There were buildings for pressing grapes and olives, and a mill for grinding wheat. The type and quality of crops varied throughout the Empire. Olives could be grown only in the warm south. Grapes were grown in southern Britain, but they were not as good as those from Spain or Italy.

RELIGIOUS CEREMONIES played a big part in the farmers' year. The Romans believed that ceremonies were just as important as sowing or plowing at the right time. In May, for example, a pig, a ram, and a bull were led around the boundaries of the fields and then killed as a sacrifice to the god Mars. The farmer would say, "Father Mars, I pray that you keep disease and bad weather away from my fields and that you allow my harvest, my corn, and my vineyard to flourish."

▷ *A Roman farm on the north coast of Africa.*

team of oxen harnessed to a mechanical harvester

beehives

wheat

OLIVE TREES were grown all over North Africa, but the olives from Tripolitania (present-day Libya) were particularly famous. They were grown on dry hillsides, above fields of wheat. The olives could either be eaten or crushed in an oil press for their rich oil.

SLAVES did most of the farm work. A trusted slave called a *vilicus* was in charge of the field laborers. They had to work very hard: if not, they might be beaten or kept in chains. Farm work was used as a punishment for town slaves whose masters thought they were lazy.

▷ *Farmers' tools were simple but effective. These knives were used for pruning grapevines.*

stables

olive press

villa rustica, *or farmhouse*

slaves' quarters

olive grove

livestock

Trade and transport

Wherever they went, the Roman armies built roads. Although they were for military use, Roman roads made it easier to transport goods on carts pulled by mules and oxen, no matter what the weather. Heavy goods were moved by water wherever possible—along rivers on barges pulled by oxen, or across the sea on merchant ships.

THE PEACE that was brought by Roman rule helped trade to flourish from one end of the Empire to the other. The demands of the wealthy also meant that luxury goods, such as silks and spices, were brought from distant lands.

△ *Coins were used throughout the Empire.*

WITHIN THE EMPIRE, the most important trade was in metals, luxury goods, and foods such as wine, olive oil, grain, and fish sauce.

Some goods were imported from beyond the Empire. Silk came from as far away as China along an overland route called the Silk Road. Spices for cooking were brought by sea from India, and incense, which the Romans burned on the altars of the gods, came overland from southern Arabia by camel caravans, or by ships sailing up the Red Sea.

KEY TO TRADE MAP

wild animals   *wild animals*   *slaves*   *grain*   *wine*   *oil*   *gold*   *metals*

▽ *This map shows where some of the goods traded around the Empire came from.*

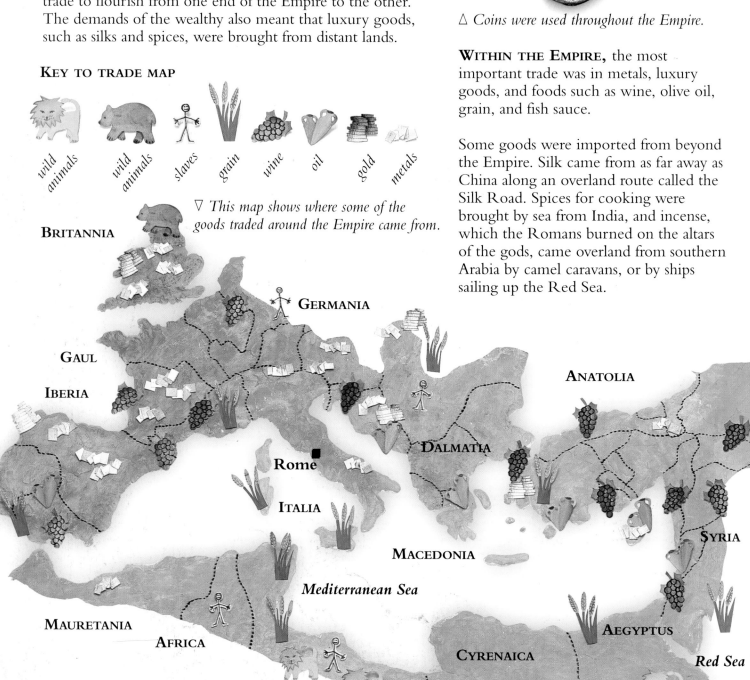

BRITANNIA

GERMANIA

GAUL

IBERIA

Rome

ITALIA

DALMATIA

ANATOLIA

MACEDONIA

SYRIA

Mediterranean Sea

MAURETANIA

AFRICA

CYRENAICA

AEGYPTUS

Red Sea

( ) ✳ **A ROMAN COIN** was like a tiny newspaper in some ways. One side was used by the emperor to announce important events, such as a military victory. He also used coins to try to win people's loyalty. The coin might show him speaking to his troops—giving people the impression that he was in firm command. Another coin might show the emperor as the chief priest, so that people would think that he had the support of the gods.

▷ *A merchant weighs some fruit using a set of scales.*

△ *Traders made healthy profits from transporting exotic animals around the Empire.*

( ) ✳ **PLINY THE ELDER** thought that foreign luxury goods were costing the Empire too much: "At the lowest reckoning, India, China, and Arabia carry off one hundred million *sestertii* a year from our Empire—such is the bill for our pleasures and our ladies."

WILD ANIMALS were brought from all parts of the Empire and from lands beyond for the games in Rome. Bears were shipped from Scotland and Ireland. Elephants came from Africa and India.

( ) ✳ **THE SAME COINS** were used throughout the Empire, making trading simple. The basic unit was a copper coin called an *as*. A larger copper coin, called the *dupondius*, was worth 2 donkeys; a bronze coin, the *sestertius*, was worth 4 donkeys; a silver *denarius* equalled 16 donkeys; and a gold *aureus* was worth 100 donkeys.

lead weight in the shape of a head

SHIPS were used to move people and goods around the Empire and beyond. As well as traveling for trade and religious reasons, some wealthy Romans went sightseeing, and some even had guidebooks.

▽ *A Roman war galley.*

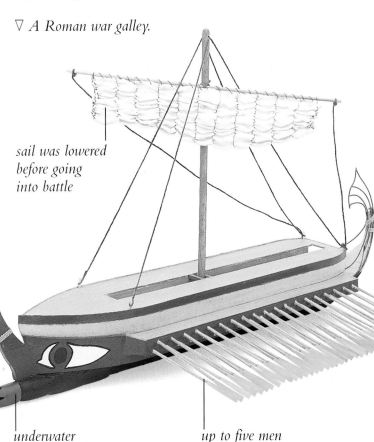

sail was lowered
before going
into battle

underwater
battering ram

up to five men
manned each oar

WAR GALLEYS were slim, fast vessels. They were powered by oarsmen who sat on benches below deck, pulling in time to orders shouted by the helmsman. At the bow, or front, there was a battering ram made of wood covered in bronze. Galleys would try to ram enemy ships in the side. Then the crew of marines (naval soldiers) would jump on board the enemy ship for hand-to-hand fighting.

PIRATES were a menace in the first century B.C. Fleets of pirates based in the eastern Mediterranean raided coastal towns and seized any ships they could. They stole the cargoes and held the crews for ransom, or sold them as slaves. In 67 B.C., the Romans gathered a fleet of war galleys and hunted the pirates down to make the sea safe.

THE SAILING SEASON lasted from March to November. Few ships put out to sea in winter because of the risk of storms, and because of shorter daylight hours. However, the city of Rome needed wheat grown abroad to feed its people, so some huge grain ships had to make the dangerous winter journey from North Africa. When grain supplies ran low in the granaries, there was panic in Rome.

IN THE SECOND CENTURY A.D., the Greek writer Lucian described the *Isis*, one of the great grain ships that sailed out of Egypt: "What a big ship! About 180 feet [55 meters] long and something over a quarter of that wide… And then the height of the mast! And how the stern rises with its gentle curve, with its golden beak, balanced at the opposite end by the long rising length of the prow, with a figure of the goddess Isis on either side!"

▽ *Merchant ships carried people, food supplies, and wild animals for the games.*

yard

foresail, or
steering sail

MERCHANT SHIPS were used to move goods around the Empire. These ships were large and round-bellied, to provide lots of storage space for all the sacks of grain and *amphorae*, or pottery jars, holding oil or wine. Because of their shape, these ships were stable but very slow. They had a big square sail on the mast with a smaller sail at the bow. Two large oars at the stern, or rear, were used for steering.

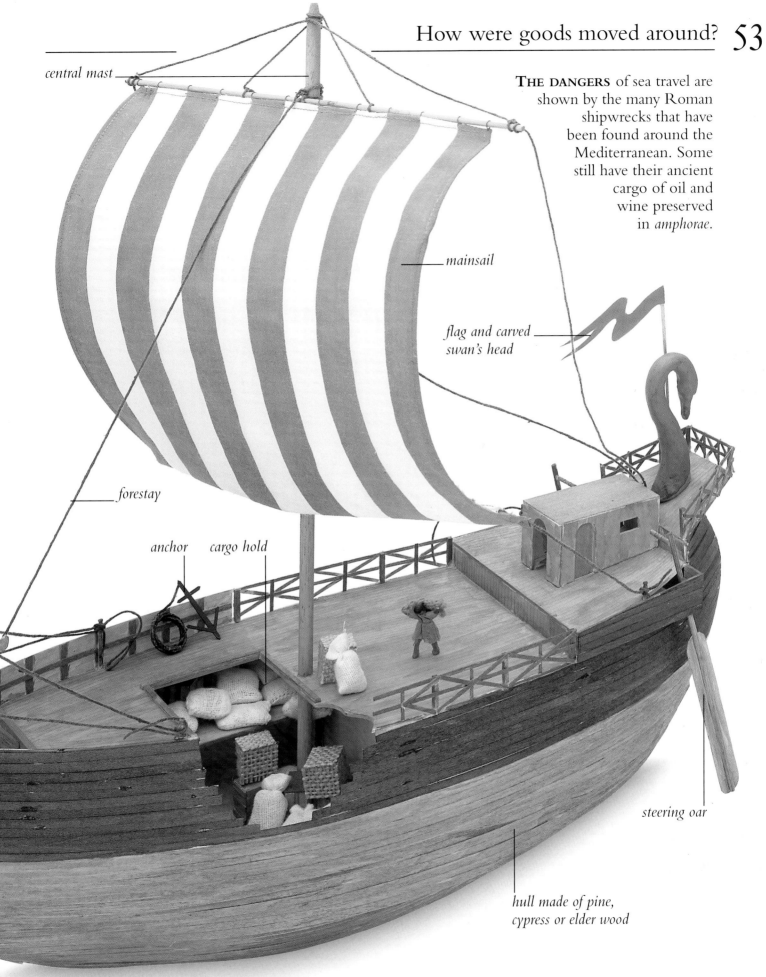

central mast

THE DANGERS of sea travel are shown by the many Roman shipwrecks that have been found around the Mediterranean. Some still have their ancient cargo of oil and wine preserved in *amphorae*.

mainsail

flag and carved swan's head

forestay

anchor

cargo hold

steering oar

hull made of pine, cypress or elder wood

The Roman army

In the first century A.D., the Roman army was mostly made up of legionaries and auxiliaries. There were 28 legions, mainly stationed around the borders of the Empire. Each one had a number and a name that was either a nickname or the place where the troops were raised. For example, the sixth legion was called *Victrix*, or victorious; and the ninth legion was called *Hispana*, or Spanish.

lionskin headdress worn over a helmet —

◁ *A legionary from the first century B.C.*

🦅 **A LEGIONARY** was a Roman foot soldier. On marches, they had to carry heavy loads of weapons, tools, and supplies. If they were not fighting or training, legionaries had to do building work. They cut down trees, quarried stone, and built roads, bridges, and forts.

▽ *A Syrian archer of the early A.D. 100's.*

Syrian archers wore long robes

△ *An aquilifer from the first century A.D.*

AUXILIARIES were soldiers who came from the provinces and who were not Roman citizens. They were poorly paid, earning only a third of the legionaries' rate. Auxiliaries fought using the familiar weapons of their own countries. Cavalry came from Gaul (France) and North Africa, slingers from islands off Spain, and archers from Syria. Auxiliaries supplied the extra fighting skills that the legions lacked.

THE AQUILIFER, or eagle bearer, carried the standard of the legion—a golden eagle on a pole. Smaller units also had standards, such as golden hands or busts of the emperor. These were used to rally the soldiers in battle. Aquilifers had to be very brave, for they led the men into the most dangerous places on the battlefield. The lionskins on their helmets were a symbol of their rank and courage.

long spear used for stabbing from horseback

▽ *A cavalry officer from the A.D. 300's.*

silver-plated helmet

▷ *A centurion from around A.D. 50.*

helmet with sideways crest

EACH LEGION had around 5,500 soldiers, including 120 horsemen who acted as messengers and scouts, keeping an eye on the enemy. The rest of the soldiers were divided into small units called centuries, each of about 80 men. Six centuries grouped together made a cohort.

silver and gold medals on chest

vine cane used to point at, or beat, the men

A CENTURION was an officer in charge of a century. To show his rank, he wore special armor made from silver-colored metal scales, and shiny greaves (shin guards). He also wore a helmet with a sideways crest as a sign of his status. He kept his men in order by beating them with a vine cane, either as a punishment, or to make them work harder.

CAVALRY played an even more important role during the later Empire, when large armies of soldiers on horseback fought alongside the legions. By the A.D. 300's, the cavalry carried long swords and round shields.

LEGIONARIES were full-time soldiers. They joined the army at about the age of 18, and had to serve for the next 20 to 25 years. It was a hard life, but it also offered security and regular pay to the poorest Roman citizens. Through good service, legionaries might be promoted to the rank of centurion. If they survived the battles they fought, they could retire and live a comfortable life.

New recruits had to swear an oath that they were free-born Roman citizens, not slaves. Sometimes, slaves tried to join the legions. If they were discovered, they were executed.

DRILLING AND MARCHING took up a large part of the legionary's day. In his book *Military Service*, the author Vegetius described the type of training program that legionaries were put through: "Every recruit, without exception, should in the summer months learn to swim, for it is not always possible to cross rivers on bridges… They should be accustomed also to leap and strike blows at the same time, to rise up with a bound and sink down again behind the shield… They must also practice throwing their javelins at the posts from a distance to increase their skill in aiming, and the strength of the arm."

MAKE A PAIR OF ARMORED SHOES

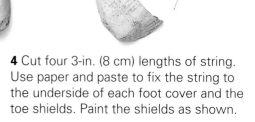

You will need: scissors, chicken wire, paper, string, flour, water, salt, paint

1 Ask an adult to help you mold the chicken wire to fit the top of your feet.

2 Make a runny paste of flour and water. Add a pinch of salt. Cover the shapes (inside and out) in layers of strips of paper dipped in the paste. Let them dry.

3 Cut off the tops of the toes as shown to make toe shields.

4 Cut four 3-in. (8 cm) lengths of string. Use paper and paste to fix the string to the underside of each foot cover and the toe shields. Paint the shields as shown.

5 Make two small holes in the sides of each shoe. Thread string through the holes and tie around your ankles.

PUNISHMENTS were harsh in the army. Soldiers who fell asleep on guard duty or ran away in battle were stoned to death. If a whole unit showed cowardice or refused to obey orders, it could be punished with decimation, which meant that one man in every ten was killed.

However, life was not all bad for a Roman soldier. At Vindolanda, a Roman fort in northern Britain, archaeologists found many letters written on thin sheets of wood. In one letter, dating from A.D. 120, a soldier complains that his unit has run out of beer!

▷ *This is a copy of foot armor that was found in the south of Italy, in an early Greek settlement.*

BAGGAGE MULES trotted alongside the marching soldiers. There was one mule for every eight men. It carried a leather tent and a millstone for grinding corn. Other mules were loaded with dismantled catapults, used for hurling stones at the enemy.

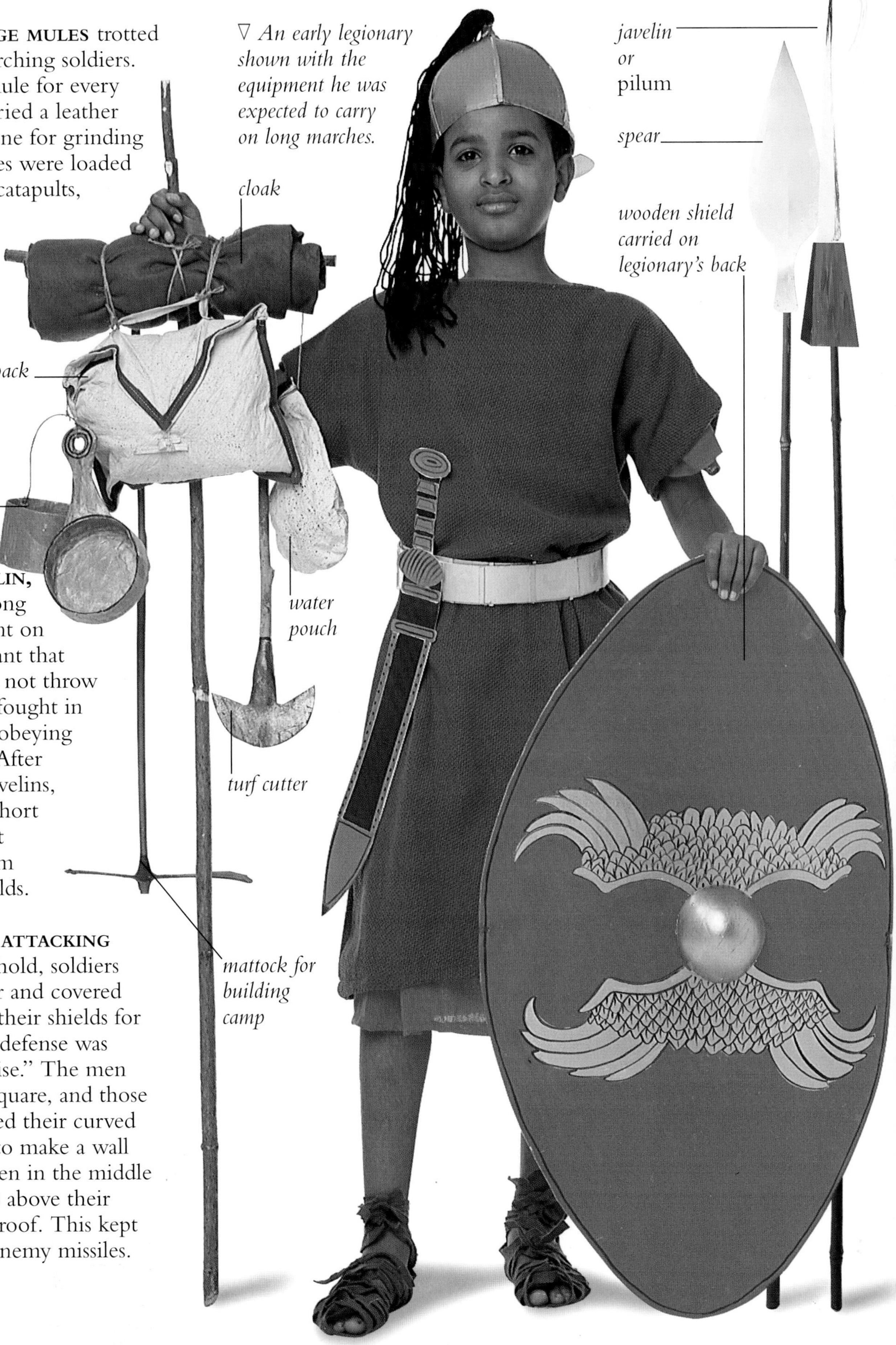

supplies carried on a wooden cross on the legionary's back

cooking pots

A JAVELIN, or *pilum*, had a long metal tip that bent on impact. This meant that the enemy could not throw it back. Soldiers fought in tight formation, obeying trumpet signals. After throwing their javelins, they drew their short swords and thrust at the enemy from behind their shields.

WHEN ATTACKING an enemy stronghold, soldiers grouped together and covered themselves with their shields for protection. This defense was called "the tortoise." The men gathered into a square, and those at the edges linked their curved shields together to make a wall of wood. The men in the middle held their shields above their heads to make a roof. This kept them safe from enemy missiles.

▽ *An early legionary shown with the equipment he was expected to carry on long marches.*

cloak

water pouch

turf cutter

mattock for building camp

javelin or pilum

spear

wooden shield carried on legionary's back

ON A CAMPAIGN, Roman soldiers slept in leather tents in temporary marching camps, which they set up at the end of each day. The rest of the time, they lived in barracks in permanent forts made of wood or stone.

FRONTIER FORTS were dotted along the borders of the Empire. They were usually manned by auxiliaries recruited from the local area, so German auxiliaries defended the Empire against German invaders. Legionaries lived some way behind the frontier, providing a second line of defense. If the front line was attacked, guards in the watchtowers would light beacons to send the urgent news.

▽ *This is a typical Roman frontier fort.*

mile castle built every Roman mile (5,000 ft. or 1.5 km) along frontiers

a main gateway

stables

barracks

workshop

FORTS changed over time, but they were often rectangular and surrounded by a ditch. Early forts were protected by a wall of timber and turf. Later, they were built with stone. Two main roads crossed the camp, leading to four gates, one on each wall. The fort was a permanent home for the soldiers, so it had to be as comfortable as possible. The soldiers always had their own baths, and sometimes amphitheaters for gladiator contests.

THE HOSPITAL was an important building in every fort, as the soldiers were often sick and sometimes injured. Military doctors knew how to reset broken bones, and they operated to remove splinters or arrowheads from wounds.

defensive ditch

THE COMMANDER'S HOUSE, or *praetorium*, was a lavish building with heated rooms where the commander lived with his family and their slaves. The business of running the legion took place in the headquarters, or *principia*. It had a strong room for the legion's money, a shrine for the standards, and a platform for addressing the troops.

IN THEIR FREE TIME, soldiers could drink beer, gamble with dice, and organize wrestling matches, horse races, and tug-of-war contests. The commanding officers preferred hunting deer and wild boar with packs of dogs.

IN MAINLAND EUROPE there were wide rivers that also acted as frontier lines. The Romans built forts and watchtowers along the west bank of the Rhine and on the southern bank of the Danube. They used them to keep an eye on the fierce German tribes across the river.

THE EMPEROR HADRIAN ordered that a wall be built across northern Britain to defend the frontier. The Romans called the people who lived north of the wall *Picti*, or painted ones, because they covered themselves in war paint.

▷ *The Emperor Hadrian ordered the building of a 73-mile (117-km) long wall, sections of which can still be seen today.*

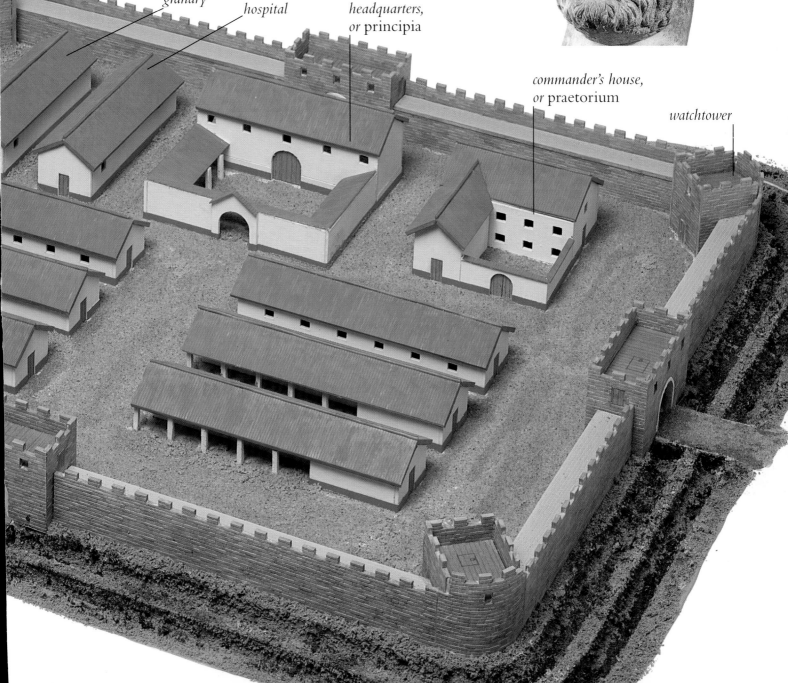

granary

hospital

headquarters, or principia

commander's house, or praetorium

watchtower

The fall of Rome

In the A.D. 300's, the Roman Empire was weakened by a series of invasions. German tribes poured over the Rhine and Danube rivers. To meet the threat, the Roman Empire was split into two halves. There was an emperor in the west, sometimes ruling from Rome, and another in the east ruling from Constantinople (Istanbul) in Turkey.

✷ **ROME WAS CAPTURED** and plundered in A.D. 410 by Alaric, king of the Visigoths. The news of the fall of the city shocked the Roman world. Jerome, a monk in Palestine, wrote to a friend: "Terrifying news has come to us from the West. Rome has been taken by assault… My voice is still and sobs disturb my every utterance. The city has been conquered which had once controlled the entire world."

△ *Many tourists visit the remains of the Colosseum in Rome.*

THE GERMAN INVADERS set up their own kingdoms in western Europe. One group, the Franks, settled in Gaul and became the French. Other German peoples, the Saxons and Angles, settled in Britain and became the English. The invaders did not usually want to destroy the Roman Empire. As a result, many aspects of the Roman way of life were kept alive in western Europe.

▷ *The title "Caesar" was used by the emperors, from Augustus to Hadrian, and by other powerful rulers throughout history.*

◁ *The eagle, once the symbol of the Roman Empire, is now a symbol of the United States and appears on the one-dollar bill. For the Romans, the eagle was the king of birds and represented Jupiter, the king of the gods, and god of the sky.*

ROMAN POLITICS AND LAW have had a lasting influence. The United States has modeled its system of government on the Roman Republic and adopted the eagle as a national emblem. Throughout history, many rulers have looked to the power and inspiration of the emperors and the Roman Empire. In some countries, rulers adopted the title "Caesar": in Russia, it became "Tzar," and in Germany it became "Kaiser."

THE EASTERN EMPIRE survived for another thousand years. It was only in 1453 that the last eastern emperor died defending his capital, Constantinople, against the Muslim Turks.

By the 1500's, the Empire no longer existed, but its influence lived on in the lands surrounding the Mediterranean in the form of architecture, language, literature, and government.

ROMAN ARCHITECTURE still influences modern buildings. Public buildings, such as banks, libraries, churches, and museums, are often modeled on Roman temples, with tall, decorative columns.

THE LATIN LANGUAGE developed into French, Italian, Spanish, Portuguese, and Romanian. Latin was kept alive in church services and writings. It also became, with Greek, an international language for scientists, who classify plants, animals, and parts of the body using Latin names.

THE MONTHS OF THE YEAR are still known by their Roman names. March, for example, is named after the Roman god Mars, and August gets its name from Rome's first emperor, Augustus. The planets are also named after Roman gods.

cyclamen
cyclamen persicum

△ *Latin is used to classify plants and species of animals.*

Glossary

amphitheater An oval-shaped Roman building without a roof. It was used for public shows, such as fights between gladiators and wild animals.

amphora A tall pottery vase with two handles used for transporting and storing wine, olive oil, vinegar, and fish sauce.

aqueduct An artificial channel, made of stone and concrete, used for carrying water from one area to another.

archaeologist Someone who searches for and studies the remains of past times, such as ancient buildings and artifacts.

atrium The entrance hall of a Roman house.

augur A religious official whose job was to find out whether the gods approved or disapproved of a course of action. The augur did this by watching the flight and behavior of birds. Many important decisions were made after consulting the sacred flock of chickens.

auxiliary Soldiers drawn from the noncitizen population of the Empire. They were paid less than citizen soldiers. On retirement, they could become Roman citizens.

barbarian A word used by the Greeks and Romans to describe foreigners.

centurion A middle-ranking Roman officer in charge of a "century" of men (80).

Chi-Rho (pronounced *Ky-roh*) A sign used by early Christians to show their faith. It combines the Greek letters *X* (Chi) and *P* (Rho), the first two letters of the word *Christ*.

circus An oval track for chariot races. The most famous was the Circus Maximus in Rome.

citizen A citizen of the Roman Empire was a full member of the Roman state, and had more rights than a noncitizen.

civilization A developed and organized group of people or nation. The Romans believed that civilization was marked by town life, laws, reading and writing, and religious ceremonies.

client A person who owed loyalty to a wealthier Roman, who was his or her patron.

consul The most important Roman government official. Two consuls were elected each year.

early imperial period The period of Roman history from 27 B.C. to A.D. 284. For most of this time, the Empire was ruled by the emperor.

emperor The ruler of the Roman Empire. The rule of the emperors was known as *imperial rule*.

equestrian A member of a class of wealthy Roman citizens. Each equestrian owned a personal fortune of at least 400,000 sestertii.

Etruscans The people who lived in northwest Italy in ancient times. The Etruscans were an important influence on the Romans.

fasces A bundle of rods, tied around an ax. An Etruscan symbol of power, adopted by the Romans.

forum The central marketplace and public meeting area in every Roman town.

freedmen and freedwomen Slaves who bought or were given their freedom. However, they did not have as many rights as free-born citizens.

fresco A type of wall painting in which paint is applied to damp plaster.

gladiator A man who fought in the arena against another gladiator or an animal. Gladiators were mostly slaves, although those that were successful were able to buy their freedom.

groma A tool used by Roman surveyors to plot straight lines, right-angles, and grids.

haruspice A religious official whose job was to predict the future or to find out the wishes of the gods. He did this by inspecting the inner organs of sacrificed animals. He also interpreted lightning and unusual events in nature, such as earthquakes.

insula A block of housing in a Roman town.

Isis An important Egyptian goddess worshiped by some Romans. She was seen by her followers as the queen of the whole universe. Isis also had specific roles as a goddess of wheat and barley, childbirth, and seafarers.

late imperial period The period of Roman history from A.D. 284 to 476. For most of this period, the Empire was divided into two halves. It also became a Christian empire.

Latin The language spoken by the Romans and the other peoples of Latium, an area in central Italy. The ancient people of Latium were called "Latins."

legionary A Roman citizen who served as an infantry soldier in a legion.

magistrate Elected official who governed the Roman state. Under the Republic, the most powerful were the two consuls. There were also the praetors, who were in charge of justice, and the quaestors, who looked after state money.

Mithras A god of light, worshiped in secret by men, especially soldiers, throughout the Roman Empire.

mosaic A picture made from hundreds of tiny pieces of pottery, stone, or glass tiles inlaid in cement.

pater familias The father and head of a Roman family.

province A large area of the Roman Empire ruled by its own governor.

provincial A native of one of the provinces of the Roman Empire. Provincials had fewer rights than citizens, but were much better off than slaves.

Roman Empire The different lands and peoples ruled by the Romans. "The Empire" also means the period when Rome was ruled by emperors, rather than by elected officials.

Roman Republic A period when Rome and the Empire were ruled by elected officials.

senators A member of the senate, a council of leading nobles who advised the consuls and the emperor. In the Empire, senators commanded the armies and governed provinces. To be a senator, you had to be elected as a member of the magistrates, and have a huge personal fortune of at least a million sestertii.

shrine A place where holy objects, such as statues of gods, were placed and worshiped. Many Romans had shrines in their homes.

standard bearer Someone who carried a pole with a flag, metal eagle, or placard on the top. Standards were used in religious processions, and as rallying points for soldiers in battle.

strigil A curved metal tool used at the Roman baths for scraping oil and dirt off skin.

stylus A penlike instrument used for writing on wax tablets.

symbol A sign or an object that stands for something else. For example, a cross is a symbol of Christianity; a lionskin headdress is a symbol of bravery.

tablinum A Roman reception room.

toga A gown worn by male Roman citizens. It was made of a single woolen sheet and wrapped around the body.

triclinium A Roman dining room with three couches in an open square for guests to lie upon.

Index